Moments in Time

Neelam Malhotra

ISBN

Hardcase 979-8-89724-514-7
Paperback 979-8-89186-829-8

Contents

• • •

Author

Neelam Malhotra, educated in Delhi University did her graduation and masters in Humanities. After a Bachelors degree in Teaching, BEd., she taught in Delhi and abroad.

But for the most part of her life she worked for an NGO, teaching in schools for the underprivileged.

Her lifelong desire to study and pursue art remained with her. After retiring from teaching she found her mentor and guru in MG Doddamani, a renowned artist and teacher. She went on to study with him. Neelam graduated in fine arts in 2023 from Hampi University.

Writing stories and poems, another personal pastime, remains a hobby she enjoys.

This book of memoirs is a compilation of her musings and remembrances. Some of the illustrations in the book are done by her.

Acknowledgements

These musings and poems were penned for myself, just something personal I enjoyed.

Like moments treasured or remembered. Till they were stolen by Naresh my husband.

Naresh colluded with Notion Press and soon began to call these writings 'a manuscript'.

Now that was a bit over the top, I confess. But the deed was done And that is how this book came about. Drawings, illustrations and vintage yellowed photographs were dug out, even borrowed from family members and added.

I have to thank my husband for his felony and for providing me a trip down memory lane.

I'm sure all our families provide us with mirth as well as heartaches, and maybe this book resonates with you in some manner.

I thank my art Guru, eminent artist MG Doddamani for his guidance to illustrate this book.

I thank my friend Jagan, himself an artist, for always, always being available to lend support or clarity.

I dedicate this book to my eccentric and lovable family and friends who may be featured somewhere in these pages. Thank you for being in my life.

Brother Farrel

Brother Farrell was an Irish missionary brother, who taught math in standard X at St. Columbus School, Delhi, in the 1950s, for about forty odd years. He was brilliant, gentle, and much loved, Tony mama's math's teacher.

Irish Brother Farrell
Of the Christian Brothers' Order
Math teacher in Std. X,
Created unwitting,
Glorious disorder.

Second period in the morning,
Punctually, without any warning
A shrouded wraith in priestly habit
He would materialize,
Like a magician's rabbit.

Those wicked, naughty boys
Mischievous irrepressible
Would be yawning
Though it be, just 8.45 in the morning.

Brother Farrel and the Wicked Naughty Boys of Std 10

"The theorem for the day..."
He would start
Amidst moaning and groaning
Horrid little rascals
Their fate, they would be, bemoaning.

For they, understood naught
Brother Farrell, he went above their heads
They'd just come to school
Tumbled out of their warm beds.

But old Brother Farrell
He would not be deterred.
He was that kind of
Hardened bird.

Excitable and passionate,
Spouting equations, theorems, formulae,
Waving chalk, before the blackboard, dancing,
In his white, priestly robes, almost prancing.

With all that whirling and twirling,
His bald pate shining, all pink and perspiring
This forelock of hair flew out
Leaving his shiny head bare.

His hairdo, a marvel!
Just this long strand of hair

The rest of his noggin bare
Round and around, he had wound.
A vainer man might despair.

Unbound, the long forelock would unravel
Over his cheek and across his face travel
Lo, a new interest in the class was born
All eyes now glued to his form.

Grinning and giggling, nudging and elbowing
Glum no more, on their lips laughter lurking
Darting eyes following the wild strand
Unabashedly smirking, the boys a wicked band.

For old Brother Farrell, was exposed
He, from his fearsome pedestal, deposed
His wound up lock in disarray,
Now made everyone smile, hurray!

Flying chalk and paper balls
Behind his back, would throw one and all
In the face, he might go red
'You.., ... You fairy', was the worst he ever said.

No longer did they wish him begone
Rather, waited every morning for him to come
For the long-plastered strand to come undone
The hilarious show would then have begun.

The beleaguered priest, a teacher so fine
Jumping and prancing, but now on the run
What a sight! A performance so divine!!
No who could be bored, this math class was such fun.

Memory of a Love Affair

A field of little light blue balls on little heads. The balls remained still when the Princi was talking, became rigid during the National Anthem, and then again began bobbing up and down with the marching.

After the open air, outdoor morning assembly, going back inside.

Hup two three, Hup two three... marching rhythmically.

Up balls, down balls... slowly disappearing into the school portals.

Little kondais on little sardar boy heads, so many together at the morning assembly. Never seen so many little boys with patkas marching together. I was wonderstruck.

Like I would be many, many times in this school later on.

I was jobless and here for an interview. My friend Anita took me to the school to meet the principal, or Princi, as he was fondly called, of Guru Harkrishan Public School, New Delhi.

My previous job at a convent school had left me shuddering. In 7 days only.

But I had a past history of convent abuse, of the strictest discipline, fright, regimen, and punishment at the hands of teachers and nuns.

I had schooled in one, The Convent of Jesus and Mary, New Delhi, from standard 1 through standard 11, the finest convent school in Delhi, to be proud of; I still am.

Forever after, for years, I hated Sunday mornings; they were a precursor to Sunday evenings and the oncoming fearful Monday mornings, the beginning of a whole week of dreaded school.

A huge majority of us hated school; we actually did.

Mrs. Jones of Standard 3, berating and brandishing her umbrella at the cleaner boy, and Miss Rondo of class 7 who doled out two or three punishments daily, the load of the written ones added another hour to the homework. But they were better than her ruler on the knuckles or legs.

English teacher Incy, Mrs. Ince, of standard 9/10/11, another one etched forever into memory. Yes, oh yes, she had three years to deflate you, unmake you, and rob you of all confidence and self-esteem.

The Hindi teacher Mrs. Aluwalia, a ghoul in a class of her own, "nikammi, nigori, angrez ki bacchi........, thi to puri angrez, ...Ingland se aatay aatay Black Sea main gir gai,......to rang kaalaa ho gayaa ...., varna thi to angrez".

We who had schooled in this Convent from a tender age, though proficient in talking in English, were not up to her standard in her subject, Hindi.

All of them were legends.

For the last three senior-most school years, one heard from Mrs Ince every day, 'Darling, how will you ever pass?',

A plaintive whine, so sad that you began to believe it. It still reverberates in my ears.

You can still find common ground with strangers who walked the hallways of the same school if you recount these names.

But the convent of recent torture was where I worked for seven days and ran away, from the tyranny of the spying nuns and the strict confinement.

I needed breathing space at school, with lungs.

Hence the interview. And the bobbing buns clinched the deal for me. Might be fun.

Made it to the Princi's office, deposited there by Anita.

G.S. Dhillon was the Principal of Guru Harkrishan Public School, New Delhi, affectionately Princi, in 1973, when I joined the school to teach the senior classes.

A serious, bearded Sardarji, dignified and wise. The twinkle in his eye was a giveaway, however.

He had to have humour, this man who ruled over a brat brigade.

A student body of more than 600 boys and girls from ages 3 to 18, comprising almost 90 percent Sikhs, a few Hindus, and fewer Christians, it was different from other schools.

The morning assembly showed rows upon rows of boys with blue patkas, their knotted hair bunned up, and girls with long ribboned plaits and almost no one with short hair.

The bigger boys sporting fresh young beards and turbans, looked like fierce, intimidating men, but were mostly large, aggressive babies.

The Principal had strong views about letting new teachers join the senior school without any experience of the junior classes.

He probably knew we needed to be eased into this school of little ruffians.

He also probably wanted to gauge our capabilities. Especially, freshly graduated young teachers, untested and just out of training, who needed to be broken in.

So, though I trained for senior classes, mandatorily, I had to teach in the junior school for three months, before graduating to the middle and senior classes. After three months, I would be moved up. With only six months of teaching experience behind me, I had no choice.

Hired, I was on the next day.

The little 3rd. standard boys and girls were not a piece of cake. They looked small, rosy, and angelic, but packed in a mean punch.

Sardars are a good-looking race. Bold and spunky, I loved these little bundles of mischief.

They arrived all neat and clean in their classrooms, having been bathed and dressed, combed, ribboned or turbaned, and shoed. Boys in white shirts, blue shorts and 'kerchief 'patkas'. And similarly uniformed, skirted girls with neat long plaits; they looked as if butter wouldn't melt in their mouths, cute and adorable.

All white and blue, disguised imps.

Days passed. I got used to the buns and plaits....

By the first break, exactly two periods later, they had fidgeted themselves sufficiently, jhuras were askew, and tendrils of hair escaped the confinement of their patkas. Belts were lopsided, laces undone, and pair plaits were no longer of the same length, having been pulled or tugged. A scratch or two appeared on shiny cheeks. Tiny welts where they had been pinched or punched.

Tight lipped, morning smiles were no longer there.

A Sikh regiment in the making.

But by the time they returned after the half break, they looked like bar brawl survivors.

God knows we teachers needed to go down for a cup of tea to regain our sanity and voices. We needed to get away.

But when we came back, all hell had broken loose.

Nobody was in class. Long, silky hair streamed down the heads of boys in shorts, who were upon each other on the corridor floor, screaming at the top of their voices. A few were bawling. A couple of weepy girls had snot running down their noses, some hiccuping tears back. All now dirty and filthy.

This was an exceptional day, the likes of which I had never seen before.

From nowhere, I heard Manjit Madam, the Hindi teacher, barking! 'Get back into class, you khotas', or donkeys. 'Get inside', she screamed.

Shaken at her ferocity, I wondered if there had been an accident.

She raised them up on their benches. So, we could see the little devils in the eye.

THIRD STANDARD KIDS AFTER THE FIRST BREAK

Now standing, the noise subsided somewhat. A few soft sobs by the girls, the boys now hard-eyed and scared.

This was their most-feared teacher.

I had to run to my own class, 3A, to teach English, for 45 minutes. The next period was free for me.

I peeked into the soundless 3B, completely silent now, still punished.

'Kee hoya, aa thennu dasan', the Hindi teacher invited me in, in Punjabi, to share the saga. 'Amarjot was teaching the class this poem. ' Oye Amarjot, tell madam what you taught the class in the break'.

The rascal, not ashamed, somewhat surprised, a little fearful, started, his body still racked with crying,

'Chai ka pyaalaa, (uh..hu),

Cheeni ki pillate, (sob..sob),

Aajaa meri darling,

meray neechay late'. (small whimpering sounds)

Unable to control myself or keep a straight face, I barely made it to the staff room to laugh aloud at Amarjot's ribald verse. He didn't even understand what he was saying ! But he had the whole class repeating it.

Manjeet, the old spinster, did and was affronted.

We were all aghast. Where did he get it?

That was my introduction to many hilarious incidents in the junior school! Even today I clearly remember Amarjot's naughty face and Manjit's thunderous voice.

A school where you could laugh, cry, and be a child.

Days later I was sent down to standard1 to stand in for an absent teacher. A dictation test had to be given.

I was to call out the words from a given sheet for the dictation.

The little earnest patkas were writing laboriously in their neatest letters, their pink tongues rolling along with the formation of the alphabet.

A dictation test is a serious matter. And hiding their work from their classmate too.

Write a word, place the sharpener to block it, write the second, and put the rubber over it. For the third word, the sharpener moved from behind to provide cover. Having run out of sharpeners and rubbers, the previous words stood shamefully exposed. I was utterly amused by this innocent charade, I watched.

Next minute, loud wails from Charanjiv in the first row.

'What happened? '

'Madamji ek to hamay aataa nahin hai, phir ye hamay dikhataa bhe nahin hai.' Sobs.

Madamji, I don't know the answer and he won't let me see his.

A crisis I did not know how to deal with... six-year-olds and their logic!

And so many laughs in the staff room, sharing the fun with my colleagues. Those school days, so different from mine, were so joyous. Children were children and were allowed to be.

What an evergreen memory to this day!

Mrs. Ince

Mrs Ince was the senior most English teacher in the Convent of Jesus and Mary teaching Std 9,10 and 11. At least two periods or an hour and a half was a daily dose of scoldings and fearful reprimands. Learning English, Shakespeare or Dickens just an adjunct.

English teacher of yore,
Mrs Ince,
You were a bore.
I have not forgotten.

Your words, you did not mince
Your voice, a wince
Moaned, almost groaned, to ask
"Darling, how do you expect to pass?"
I have not forgotten.

White haired, sagging boobs
Tall, the shoulders a droop,
A faded dress
No smile, ever, in your address
Not forgotten

Dickens
MRS INCE
Smith

Looked at us with a baleful stare,
This motley crowd came in my share,
Put in our places, we were
Being kind to us did not occur.
I have ......not forgotten

Mrs Ince, you droned on and on
Shakespeare squirmed,
Dickens groaned
The students moaned.
I have not forgotten.

The butterflies outside,
Playfields calling
And us
Parse and phrase
Write and rewrite.

Our youth caged
We sat through diatribe.
Lectures and all
Homework, class work, all
Bore bore bore
English teacher of yore
Stole my time
Youth and all
I have not forgotten.

Mothers

It all started with Dai, my grandmother.

If the word 'Grand' prefixed to any mother applies to anyone, it applies to her. My Grandmother was really and truly grand.

A grand matriarch of a three generational clan, of unruly bold sons, frontier men, born in pre partition India, in Dera Ismail Khan, a district in North West Frontier Province. The next generation was of children born to them in a different land, in divided India, educated in convents and missionary schools.

And then great grandchildren who could not even speak or understand their native Derawali dialect. Little foreign pigs, lovable automatically, by being hers.

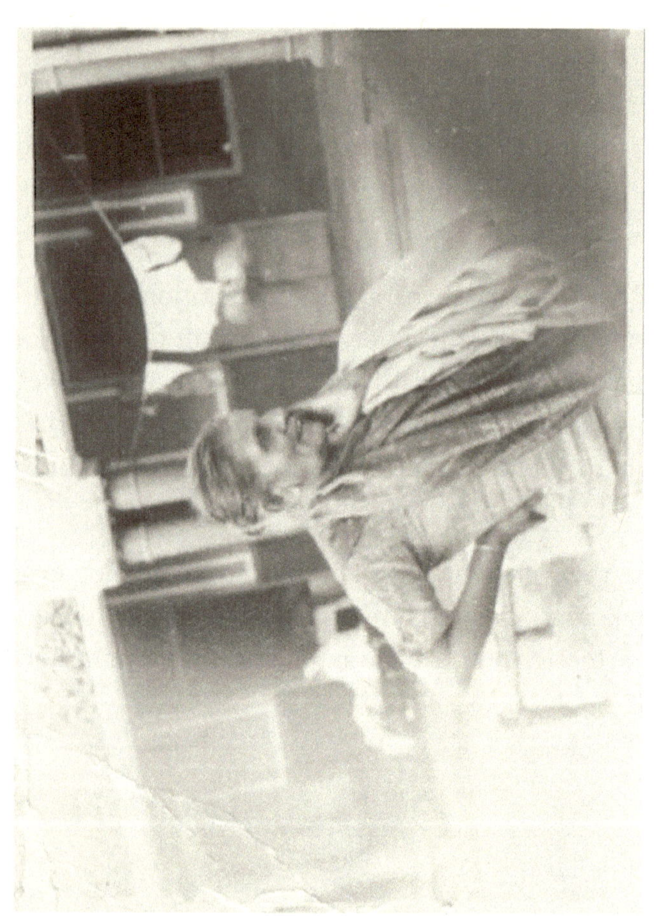

Dai set the tradition of the Mothers. She was a beautiful strong, positive, cheerful, woman, protective of her family, decisive, a breaker of tradition. A feminist before the word was coined.

Like, she wore what she pleased. Printed bras and matching printed petticoats, under see-through mulmul sarees and blouses.

My tiny devout Nani, mom's mother, who was always seen murmuring prayers through trembling lips, was scandalized.

Dai took the lead in family matters, she ruled, not her husband, my grandfather.

Dai took care of everyone's needs. She could not bear to see her own in distress and if required took bold measures to alleviate it.

It was she who arranged matrimonial alliances of her sons and daughters.

She bore three daughters and three sons to her husband, our Lalaji, my grandfather. She was his capricious beautiful young wife.

Always ailing with a multitude of sicknesses, prematurely old, half blind, Lalaji could not manage the family businesses. That was left to his brothers and subsequently his young sons.

Grandfather, though an angel mostly, was a man of vile temper, losing it sometimes. Once he threw a bunch of keys at her in anger, hurting her head. The vixen in her would pretend to leave him, hiding like a child somewhere behind the door.

To her glee he would go stumbling after her, fearing she had run away.

The family business of wholesale spices and merchandise itself was in jeopardy when the partition of India took place. The family fled during the bifurcation of India, in the aftermath of the killings, lootings, the fires that consumed the town of Dera Ismail Khan, on the Jhelum river, land of our forefathers, our roots and traditions.

The women and children had been evacuated to a safe place, our Dharmsala in Haridwar, months earlier, as refugees, in the yet undivided India.

Menfolk, a few, were left behind in Dera Ismail Khan in the hope that families would return if things normalized. One young man from each business family stayed back, guarding the home and wealth. Not distinguishable from one another, or the adversary, all the young men sported beards, wore shalwar kurta, the national dress of the frontier Pathans, and carried guns to defend themselves.

Civilians forced by circumstances to defend their land, in very unsafe times in history.

Things got worse by the day. Daily, news filtered in, of dreadful murders and lynchings. Excesses and brutality prevailed equally on both sides. There was no hope of returning to their homes in Dera for the refugees who had travelled out to Haridwar or Amritsar.

The partition of India and Pakistan became a reality.

The few young men left to guard their homes and shops had scant chance of getting out of Dera safely, amid the rioting and killing that was happening everywhere.

One such was my father, Kanwarbhan.

Dai appeared before the family elders, her husband's brothers, all now safe in the bhavan in Haridwar.

Her head bowed and covered, she declared that she would not eat another morsel of food till her elder son, my father, was brought out of Dera Ismail Khan. All the elders were safe and here, yet her son was guarding the family hearth, and business.

At the risk of his life.

She would not hear of it. She had already lost her elder son and a daughter, who died in childbirth. She could not lose another.

Securing him seemed next to impossible at that time. The elders hawed and hummed. Granny was adamant.

A British pilot, a mercenary, a bold daredevil, who flew sorties into the troubled land, on rescue missions, amid the fires that consumed their burning homes, was engaged.

He returned that evening, mission unaccomplished; he could not land his aircraft amid the raging fires of the city.

It was too dangerous!

Dai took matters into her own hands. Her son was lost to her, maybe forever!

She promised the pilot her entire jewellry, that of her three daughters - in – law's and her own, considerable by any standards, which she had secreted out of Dera. Two bottles of whiskey and all her jewelry, in a bundled cloth was given by her to the pilot, at the airfield, where she rushed off to, imploring him to bring back her son.

He needed to get quite drunk to undertake that outrageous, Hollywood-war-movie-type, rescue mission. I would have promptly fallen in love with him, had I been around. I'm quite sure he must have looked like Gregory Peck or Clint Eastwood.

Successful this time, he heroically delivered, and, my father was home.

But Dad was the second son.

Her eldest, Navnit was a gentle poet, a philosopher, a seeker of answers. His seeking led him astray, his answers he misunderstood.

KANWARBHAN

Padma & Raj

A beautiful tender wife of 26 years, two little girls, one just an infant, he left behind, that awful day when he took his life. The agony and the trauma of my family can never be comprehended, that heard a gunshot, and found a dead son, killed by his own hand.

This incident remains shrouded in mystery, it was a painful subject, a taboo; the enigma still haunts us.

Even as the shock receded, Dai declared that her young widowed daughter-in-law, Shakuntala, be treated like her eldest son. In every manner, like a son, in inheritance, in position and respect.

Shakuntala's two daughters were hereafter never to be considered fatherless.

Unheard of in those days when women did not have equal rights, widows none, Dai made sure Shakuntala, our Bari Mummy, never lacked for anything.

When her own were in distress Dai rose up like Durga, the Protector goddess, herself.

And Bari mummy's two daughters, Raj and Padma are probably the most universally loved girls of the family, beloved by all.

Dai was not always right in what she decided. But she took responsibility for her actions and her decisions.

Anchi And Allo

Then there were Anchi and Allo, her two daughters. Her two daughters, were not married into wealthy families.

Probably lacking even in basic needs.

Alliances were decided not merely for the sake of the

offsprings' happiness. Caste, sub-caste, associations in society, obligations, all nebulous pulls and pushes decided your fate. You were promised away on a whim; that was your lot.

Sometimes even before you were born.

But her girls Anchi and Allo were not happy.

In her wisdom, Dai proclaimed that they would live with her.

More with her, lesser with their in-laws, along with their children and...., even their husbands were welcome.

No separation, just change of residence.

No one could question her. Not even the sons-in-law.

Or her sons. Or Lalaji, my grandfather.

She would provide for them. And out of the family coffers, she did. And our young aunts lived with us along with their children, our cousins in one huge happy joint family.

Lily

Lily was my most beautiful aunt, seventeen, not even out of her teens.

Dai, while sitting in the garden spied this pretty teenage girl walking home from the college across the road. She would see her going past, often.

Who was this lovely girl? And Dai followed her to her destination, followed her to her grandmother's house.

Ulterior in her motive, finding her most desirable for her young son Manohar, my uncle.

Bold and whimsical as she was, Dai asked for her hand and it was granted. She became my beloved Chachi or younger aunt.

Happiness was not the lot of my Uncle and Aunt. There was incompatibility, no one could do anything about it.

But Dai was protective of her youngest daughter-in-law, never tolerating any criticism of her. The differences between Lily and Manohar were their own matter.

'She's so young,....... she'll learn, she's just a child'........,

The 3 Mothers In The Background Shakuntala,

Krishna And Lily

She made all the excuses for her. Never any censure in the days when mothers-in-law were fearlessly mothers-in-law.

No one raised a voice after she had spoken. No one took sides.

Lily Aunty remained our loved youngest mother of the clan, the other two being Shakuntala our Bari Mummy and Krishna, my mother. All three sisters-in-law.

Dai called her daughters-in-law 'bachara', or child, as she called us all.

Till her very sad end Lily remained a loved daughter of the house, even though she and my uncle found no togetherness. All three mothers were equally loving to all the children of the household, I never felt the difference between their love.

Krishna my mother was often sick, then Bari took over the kitchen. If my mom was strict, I took cover behind Lily. They were all my mothers. Their differences, if any were not aired in public, and did not make an iota of difference of our trust in them.

The young daughters-in-law entered their joint family homes early, at age 15 or 16, and 17, then who did they learn from? The head of the household, Dai.

For Dai, all the children were special. Tutored and schooled in her ways, the young daughters-in-law grew to care for all in the big joint family.

Joint families were unparalleled socialistic institutions where resources were shared, children nurtured, elders revered and assisted through old age, the less fortunate provided for, a maternal and material blanket spread over all.

If the head of the family was enlightened, this was a sanctuary for everyone.

That Lily, my Aunt and her husband, my Uncle, were estranged never mattered, while Lily lived in our big joint family. As young people in the family, we were a little oblivious to their distressing life.

Dai made sure Lily was provided for abundantly, never insecure about her position in the household.

One day upon returning from school I found Dai as usual in the front garden, sitting on a charpoi, a light, portable wooden bed, in the gentle December sun, plucking the leaves off the spinach stalks. We'd be having 'saag' or spinach for dinner for sure.

She asked about my school day. Sports Day was round the corner and I was taking part in the relays. 'Oh, so you can run fast?', she exclaimed, 'come race me then '.

Dai jumped off her charpoi and raced around our big lawn, with all of us, kids, chasing her. She ran fast at the ripe old age of 70 years. Finally gasping, she flopped into the cot, with all of us atop her, laughing and being hugged.

Saag in our home was black, not green as spinach is, made in an iron wok, full of fragrant ghee and simple spices. Mouthwatering in its very memory!

It was to be eaten with phulkas, big puffed rotis dripping with more ghee.

One of the mothers made the phulkas, and if they weren't perfect, fully round and inflated like little footballs, they would be rejected by Lalaji, our grandfather. She would be in the doghouse.

Grandfather, who would be fed first, would refuse to eat them; they would be chucked, flying out of his thali.

Another mother would be called in to produce perfect footballs. The daughter- in -law who made the ones to his satisfaction would be rewarded, ie., deputed with the honour, or onerous job, of feeding the difficult man, forever after.

It would of course change occasionally. If a pulka got burnt or was too thick she too would be out of favour and demoted.

Wasn't that fun? Woohoo woooo, off phulka duty for a while.

Sometimes I think Bari Mummy and Krishna Mummy did this on purpose, to get a rise out of their strict father-in-law.

And then giggle mischievously beneath their pallu -covered heads.

The good wife Dai would be sitting beside Lalaji, fanning him, with her big hand fan, while he ate. She was smiling. She could see through their charades, but the girls were also her little ones.

When my father built the new house in Delhi, Dai wanted grape vines planted along the boundary wall. The little grand children would pluck the sweet grapes, eat them, sticky juice dribbling down their chins, dirty and sweet themselves, she daydreamed. Yearning for a house overrun by playing little ones, Grandmother envisioned early, what she wanted her big home to be like.

She appropriated the central room for herself, from where she could see the comings and goings of all the members of her brood, growing and blossoming. Who came from school, who had been fed, who was late, which one needed care...been crying? Hurt?

She was the most important figure of the large family, the heart of the loving web she had fashioned.

Even the grand sons-in-law felt her presence. The eldest grand son-in-law, Upinder, was a UK educated smart young man. He intrigued her, with his western ways. So she promptly dared him, 'kiss your wife in my presence and I give you a hundred rupees note'.

Which he slyly did and made a cool hundred, my Didi Raj blushing.

The second grand son-in-law, Ashok, had her blessing to court her granddaughter Padma, long before the others in the family accepted him. In times gone by marriages were arranged and finding your own mate, a college friend or a colleague was considered a bit scandalous.

But Dai approved, almost a co - conspirator. Ashok was the right one, only because her granddaughter loved him. The happiness of her granddaughters was very dear to her. She could think wisely, ahead of many.

Some years on, through all the travails of his health, Grandfather, our Lalaji passed away. A gloom descended over the household. The elders mourned, the children fell silent. After the cremation, someone, whispered, ' so this year we will not be celebrating Diwali? '

Dai, looked up, and through her sorrow spoke. Looking around at all assembled, she said, 'we will celebrate, may my grandchildren live long, they are here with me, we will celebrate.'

We lit crackers, she sat far, not with us in spirit, her mate of many years gone like a breeze. In his illness he was her responsibility, but in his absence, her soulmate.

Her sorrow she never shared, for she was the light and life of that castle, where she was Queen. She was there only to provide a big welcoming heart to all hers who needed her, who were in trouble, or sorrowed, or were hungry in any manner.

When she lay sick herself, we were not allowed to feel sorry.

Dai was mischievous. A big window was always open behind the headboard of her bed for she loved air and light. The window opened to a little-frequented part of the outdoors of our house.

For her ailments, her heart, her arthritic knees, Chacha gave her a cocktail of tablets. With her left hand she would hold a glass of water, and in her right hand, the hated handful of pills. The right hand would aim the tablets at her open mouth, all altogether, but actually out of the window just behind her, and then the glass of water drunk studiously, swallowing each pill painfully, with great artifice. Oh, how she hated her medicines!

But one day she was caught out, when someone spotted a heap of pink and white pills lying outside.

'Oh, must have been one or two that went out by mistake,' she innocently proclaimed. She knew how to wriggle out of her mess.

Never one to moan or groan, I bet she found it confining to be struck down with ailments. Independent till the end, even to the last day, she gave herself a bath, made her own dinner. Declining to eat with her daughters-in-law, who now had split from the main kitchen and had their own menageries, she made all her own meals.

The first food of the day was always an offering to Shinaji, Krishna's avatar, our family God. She only ate what she offered Him, prasad. That surely could not be cooked in any of the newer kitchens where the strictest rules of Vaishnav food were not followed, which meant no meat, no onions, garlic, or unwashed bodies wandering around.

We, little unbathed grubbies were always there, our greedy hands in some biscuit tin.

A big family tightly bound together with love, where everyone was individually cared for, selflessly nurtured, is the legacy she left behind.

That is why it was so hard, and still is, for everyone to go their own way. She held us so tightly, so well and so long that breaking away is impossible.

It's like breaking up everyone.
Dai, Mother and Grandmother!

ALLO BUA WITH RAJ & DAI WITH PADMA

Bua My Allo Bua

Allo, the youngest of Dai's, my grandmother's six children, my Allo Bua, was my father's youngest sister and my aunt, and Granny's favorite child. Everyone knew it.

Otherwise how was it that she was allowed to get away with....almost anything short of murder.

Pretty as a peach, joyful, wayward, witty and spirited, she ruled her father's roost.

She had an unruly tongue, spoke her mind, said things women did not say those days, abused and swore, left my Mother and my elder Aunt shocked and speechless. Her own elder sister Anchi in a faint!

Delighted at her profanity, the cousins and relatives whispered her shockers and laughed, always greedy for newer scandalous ones.

She would wear one sister-in - law's new saree, another's jewels or some newly - gifted sandals, from Lahore, the fashion capital, without so much as 'by your leave'.

And if something got spoilt or misplaced....torn or broken, she felt no compunction.

She was just having innocent fun. So spoilt was she in her father's house, and how!

She got married soon enough and had to be banished to another's house.

Parsotlal was Bua's husband. She suffered him for he was not of a fine wealthy family like her father's. He was a merchant of long cloth, raw and unbleached, the kind that comes in bales and is used for heavy duty work, like sofa -making, before being overlaid by finer upholstery.

In the fashion of his cloth, he too seemed uncouth and unbleached, and not of her class, to Bua.

The very spoilt, fashionable princess of her father's house that she was, her clothes, her shoes, her demeanour, sense of fashion, all were let down by this simple man.

She had expected more of life. He could not rise to her expectations, she bore him three children, but she never stooped to become like his family.

Years passed...

She was more in her mother's house, where she raised her two children. My cousins were a little older.

Bua spent her life matching and reading horoscopes, visiting astrologers, priests and fortune tellers, trying to make sense of her own life and everyone else's.
She never wore her misfortunes on her face, though. Never woeful.

Bua, Allo Bua, my aunt was always around, as I remember my childhood.

She was there, as my mother's eyes, if my mother needed the purest almond oil pressed from almonds 'before your very eyes', in a manner of speaking, from the cold pressing machine.

She was there, cooking, when Krishna Janam Ashtami prasads were cooked in huge vessels, so that loaded thals, or platters of sweetmeats could be sent as gifts to married daughters' homes.

She was there, whether you had thought of it or not, with an astrologer to read your teenage daughter's horoscope. And if the 'horror scope' was the harbinger of bad news, like there's another five years before she finds a match, she was there to get the priest to do poojas, and upayas or remedies to brighten her matrimonial prospects.

Her astrological predictions were exciting. Always, like the next episode of the latest TV serial. Couldn't wait to know.

This nephew would do 'bijnus', business, and become rich.

That one would amount to nothing, but have enough for the basics, 'dal, roti'. Poor boy!

One niece would suffer a divorce because her 'Lacchans', or her wicked, bad ways. Poor kid probably received some boy's phone calls at the worst.

The other one would sadly settle abroad however much you didn't want her to. Settling abroad those days was like 'kala pani', or exile and banishment, to the Andamans, the prison for lifers.

It was a time before connectivity, for if you went beyond the 'seven seas', you went forever, you'd be given up for dead.

All of us had 'patris', our horoscopes made by her current favorite pandit, the one whose predictions she found palatable.

Strange books with stranger crisscross diagrams, stars sitting in houses and not in the firmament, indecipherable.

Unverifiable too. No one pandit would agree with another's readings or predictions.

Anyway, their mumbo jumbo, for they always spoke in riddles, could only be understood by Bua.

Most afternoons her matinee show was spent in some far off temple, hanging on the words of the pandit/ astrologer where she reached changing three buses and returned late, spent of both money and energy, bursting with readings from the 'horror scopes'.

My mother, and the other mothers in our large joint family were treated to the evening show, listening to the latest predictions, hanging on her every word. As if the family misfortunes, or their aversion, was in her hands. She definitely thought so.

A victim herself too ......

I vividly remember the day she burst into the gates of the family home, breathless, her rotund frame heaving, slipperless and crazy eyed. She flopped down on the first cot in Grandmother's room, and began groaning, 'hai.. hai.. hai', ...an awful sound from her, and then thrashing about, flailing arms and legs.

Water, food, tea, all were refused.

This continued till 4 pm.

The doctor came and went because she wouldn't see him. And he couldn't deal with nebulous demons within her. The family hovered around helplessly, to no avail. Was it the end?

By 5pm she came round, accepted a cup of tea, something to eat, and found her tongue. Rather the tongue found her and miraculously now there was no other symptom of distress, just an uncontrollable tongue, her friend and foe.

"Eh bebakhtaa, sanyaan moiyaa, lurr vanjay, garanday marnee, sirr saraay tayda, bhaa lagee......".

With her trademark 'bujjas', fingers splayed, palms outstretched aggressively in your face, she blazed again and again, raving.

Matching curses with bujjas, 'you luckless fellow, of loved ones dead, may you drown, all your family perish, your head catch fire, be engulfed in flames....'

Nothing special.
Standard Derawala fare..... not any worse than usual.... these were the regular abuses. We'd heard her use them about all the time. Delicious! Matchless!!

In no other language do they sound so delightful and gladden my heart as they do in Derawali!

Somebody was getting the choicest abuses, his ancestors and coming generations were not spared either. Cursed again and again, consigned to the flames, or the swirling waters of the river, the deepest whirlpool, set upon by writhing worms; a whole lot of unnamed folks were sent to their doom.

Not once, not even twice, poor things, but over and over again. Maybe even sequentially by the flames, water and creepy crawlies.

The humour of her drama didn't escape her. She could always laugh at herself, but later. It would become a family story to be savoured again and again.

Another hour gone, when coherence dawned, one gathered that the astrologer was being cursed along with his entire lineage, of now, and of those yet to come.

He had predicted her end precisely, to the month, date and the hour, years ago.

She, through the years, had carried the Damocles sword over her head.

But just that morning, listening to the devotional kirtan in the temple, while in a mood of religious joy, she suddenly remembered, with fearful panic, that it was the month, the day and the time of her predicted demise!!

Undone, she ran home, 2-3 kilometers, like a woman possessed, along the way losing her slippers and purse, house keys and hairpins, along with her sanity.

By five she realized the fearful hour had passed, she was still..... breathing!

She was in fact sitting up in bed. Safe.

By the end of the evening she was almost her own self. She just wanted to be sure she would be up and kicking the next day. Kicking the astrologer, viciously.

Next morning her sense of humour got the better of her, and the previous evening became a joke to be shared.

She could laugh at herself mercilessly. The joke life played on her, she played it back.

It didn't cure her of going to the astrologers however, she found newer ' better' ones. With more bizarre predictions.

Pateshwar

Our Kitchen Mother

Pateshwar, our family cook, genial and motherly, never failed to make everyone their favorite dishes. He was always toiling away in the vast kitchen of our joint family. Paneer for the children, the humble custard for Chacha, his newest panacea for gastric afflictions, or galolas, the ghee laden delicacy which was anything but delicate; this marvelous cook had different palates to please.

In fact galolas made one look quite 'undelicate' if enjoyed often.

So, when Allo Bua had to have her wisdom tooth extracted, all wisdom deserted her prior to the eviction of the tooth, though the tooth itself was still within her. Fear, extreme fear took over.

Pateshwar was instructed to make 'seera' or halwa with extra ghee, to give strength before the major surgery. Only Allo Bua knew of the magical healing properties of ghee, or 'ghiu', along with Grandmother, and the elder Bua, Anchi.

The daughter's-in-laws did not, for they were aliens, nincompoops, having being imported from another house.

Pateshwar dutifully laid the seera or as he pronounced it, 'halua', before the suffering patient. In extreme pain but definitely with pleasure, it was consumed.

Within the hour Allo Bua presented herself to Dr Jaina, everyone's dentist. Everyone's and for everything dental.

No speciality excluded.
His enlarged portrait along with pictures of molars and incisors, was pasted outside his clinic wall in Chandni Chowk, in old Delhi or Purani Dilli. He was the man of the mouth. But even he knew when he was beaten.

So fearful was Bua, that her shaking and shivering convinced the doctor he faced a doomsday situation. He sent her back, to come another day.

More halwa, with more ghee, by Pateshwar.

This time the halwa did the trick. She held out till the extraction of the wise little tooth, that must have been relieved to have heard the last of the wailing.

But the rest of Allo Bua got home in great pain, a swollen cheek, held together by three yards of pallu of her saree, twisted into a little crushed ball.

Seera, Pateshwar, 'I can eat nothing else, just some soft, extra soft seera with generous amounts of 'ghiu'. It was made fresh, dripping with ghee, the fat of all fats, superior. The qualities of ghee are altogether another big story. Known to Buas and Grandmothers genetically, and later to Mothers, by tutoring.

(Tho' not relevant to the matter at hand it is a sure shot miracle recipe, straight from the lost Archives of Cures. The purest of pure Ghee, a heaped tablespoon at least, boiled in milk with quantities of crushed almonds, sugar, cardamom, and turmeric, can cure almost any affliction if availed of, at least once a week. Promise.

Thought I'd share this, 'one remedy for all maladies', while on the subject of ghee.)

The Halwa or Ghee, whichever you wish, was consumed painfully this time. I've no doubt she was in pain.

But Pateshwar was by this time cross eyed with puzzlement.

"Ye kaisa daant hai, Buaji ka ? Nikalwanay se pahlay bhi halua, nikalwanay ke baad bhi halua !"

What kind of tooth of Buaji's is this, that needs halwa before, and halwa after extraction?

The gentle cook didn't dare to be amused; she was very prominent in our family.

He merely wondered at the wonderful properties that halwa bestowed on errant molars under eviction.

How could he ever know it was the 'ghiu'?

Parsotlal

Bua's Husband

Allo Bua did not care for her husband. Ofcourse she looked after him, always.
But he did not gladden her heart. She wanted to soar high, in the air, but found him firmly parked on the ground, too close to earth.

Of long winded speech, Parsotlal was a man of unparalleled obstinacy, no laughter, no joy. He was as boring and dull as she was luminous as light, and full of life and laughter.

You might fear her whiplash tongue or her outstretched palm-in-the-face 'bujjas', an absolute indictment and insult to the recipient, if you crossed her path.
But they were never for her loved family, brothers, sis-in -laws, children of the family.

She loved us to a fault, we were above criticism.

But the luckless 'bebakhtaa' husband was an alien creature. To be cursed regularly, to no avail. He remained consistent like dough.

How could you spend a lifetime with dough?

She found him good for nothing. Not even for a joke.
Mercifully his two children were hilarious.
For Allo it was a no go, at the most a 'suffer-each-
other-marriage'. And she suffered him.

Parsotlal drew up his chair next to the watchman at
the gate to watch passing traffic Yes, on the pavement,
just watch passing cars and buses, bikes and school
children. For hours. Simple joys of a simple man in
old age.

Upon returning from the temple and finding him so
parked at the gate, enjoying his inane activity, Bua got
so incensed, she burst out',
" Hai hai, have you nothing better to do? Why doesn't
the police come and take you away?"

Were we all scandalized and shocked!! Oh boy!
Which lady in those days was ready to consign her
master to the lockup? She had an acerbic tongue.

And years later she declared to shock and amuse us
further,
"I would have divorced him, but divorce was unheard
of those days".

By evening it had become a big joke, this scandalous
uttering of hers!
She was mirthfully relating it to all her young nieces
and nephews, unrepentant.
Quite aware of the example she was setting. Somewhat
wild as she was always wont to be.

In the general merriment, I don't think Parsotlal, uncomprehending as he always was, realized he was the butt of the joke.

And we, young as we were, did not understand she was sparring, almost laughing at her own fate.

The Two Nanis

Parvati, my Nani, my mother's mom, and Ramrakkhi, her sister, were both very fair, pretty, diminutive, about 4' 7" tall, and very, very devout. You could see the halos around their heads, almost.

When Ramrakkhi visited my Nani Parvati from Amritsar, the devotional quotient scaled a different high altogether. She would stay for a few months. They would pray together, meditate together, eat together, and sleep in the same room. They were almost twins in their good looks and angelic demeanor.

Nani's temple had an entire room on the mezzanine floor. It had a low, low ceiling, about four feet or a little more. One entered, head bowed, so as not to get a bump; and by default, automatically respectful. My dad, of six feet, would be doubled over, in divine prostration, without an iota of piety, if ever he visited.

He never did, though, for he was a devout atheist.

The Thakurjis or Gods were in a wooden 'pangeeree', a small wooden throne. All the brass and silver figurines of Ramji, Lakshmanji, Sitaji, Shivji and Parvatiji, baby

Krishna and Nandiji, and others stood in the satin-lined pangeeree.

They were bathed, hand-scrubbed daily, and shone till they gleamed like pure gold, clothed, jewelled, and garlanded.

And then offered 'bhog', a food offering that became pershaad, or prasad.

To be distributed among all, just a sweet morsel, a blessing from Thakurji.

We, kids at that time, would be little beggars just waiting for a peda, or meethi boondi. The bhog was different every day. It could be bananas or apples, chopped up. On special days, like when Nani did Satnarayan Pooja, it was churma of wheat flour, atta roasted in ghee with nuts, or just Mithai from the sweet shop.

Oooo, the divine aroma of churma roasting would be all over the house. The kids knew pershaad was special that day; alongside, they also learnt about special auspicious Hindu days.

Sometimes, in greedy anticipation, on holidays, they sat through the monthly Satnarayan Katha. The Kathas were stories told, by which you actually learnt about events far back in ancient history, so far back that they had become myths, in which good always triumphs over evil, and in which praying to God saves you from all the tragedies and travails of life.

At night, Thakurjis would be put to bed. Lain down and covered with a tiny cosy blanket. Good night was sung to the tinkling of the small brass handbell.

Obediently, the Thakurji's allowed themselves to be tucked in, and without story telling or arguments about sleep time, they instantly went to sleep.

You see, they were completely in Nani's control; any mother would have envied her ideal parent-child relationship.

They were so good, and she was so devoted to them.

Next morning, at the crack of dawn, the Thakurjis woke up to the tinkling of the ghanti, Nani's bell.

Their ablutions were so thorough that all the Thukurjis gleamed. Rubbed and wiped vigorously to become eyeless, noseless, and round-faced, eroded mercilessly.

After Nani felt she had sufficiently polished or punished them; she allowed them to shine divinely.

They seemed to be smiling beatifically, but you couldn't be sure because they were featureless after the beauty treatment and the daily exfoliation.

Thakurjis were now on duty, on call, to hear prayers, bestow favours, bless whoever came with a request or just in devotion.

My Nani would then sit down with her daily prayers and meditations. With mala beads in hand and the constant murmuring of the mantras, she spent many hours in her temple, sometimes nodding off, and then waking up to start again.

No one knew when she would emerge from the mandir.

So, when Ramrakkhi Masiji and Nani entered the mandir together, their meditations grew longer and longer. They would enter, freshly bathed, with wet, long, streaming hair, and sit down alongside with their rosaries or mala beads.

Hours would elapse, and the angelic duo remained motionless. However, if you spied diligently, Nani might look sideways, with a barely open eye, to see her sister still praying. Swiftly, she would avert her face and stoically continue. Minutes later, the other sister would check out her companion, in competition to see who lasted longer.

This went on to the exasperation of the three daughters-in-law, downstairs.

The two Nanis had not eaten a morsel, and it was getting to be one o'clock in the afternoon. The eldest daughter-in-law, mother to all, thus called Jhaijee, would send the middle one, Savitri, with two big silver glasses full of milk. But who could disturb such devotion?

Milk returned.

Half an hour later, the youngest one, Nirmal, milk reheated, was sent up but returned with a woeful expression.

They weren't finished yet.

And they continued to look beatific, matching the silent splendour of the gods across them, glowing like the Thakurjis themselves, sitting in the pangeeree, and Nanis outside the pangeeree.

Meanwhile, the three daughters-in-law had lunch to prepare. Their three husbands, my Mamajees, Mom's brothers, had to be sent off to the shop, the wholesale fabric business of the family. My mamas had lunch before leaving.

And thereafter, the brats had to be fed, some thirteen of us and two young aunts, mother's younger sisters, my loving masis.

It was a school holiday. My two brothers and I, the eldest daughter's offspring, went to Nanighar, or Nani's house. We were visiting our cousins to play the day away.

Time was a luxury to be whiled away, not valued. 'Quality time' was not even a concept then.

The kids were playing noisily, 'Dark Room', in the middle of the day, in a room with curtains drawn to block out all the light, all laughing and giggling.

When the blindfolded den came upon someone hiding in the darkened room he had to identify and name the person. It became a guessing game. Sometimes you couldn't tell, Rajiv from Sunil; they all were thin and gangly.

The Dark Room Players

A nose would be pulled or scratched.

Very soon, a fight would erupt; it always does when kids are hungry. Lunch was far away.

The two seniors, my Nani Parvati and her sister Ramrakkhi, had not even had breakfast!

What were they to do? Jhaijee, Savitri, and Nirmal could grumble silently, but to no effect.

The Nanis emerged from their meditations with the thali of pershaad, to the relief of some and the joy of others.

Dark Room forgotten, the motley bunch of us, crowded around greedily to get their pershaad, with cupped hands outstretched.

Milk appeared again, and the two saintly ladies could no more pretend they weren't starving; they drank it; their fast was happily broken.

Now Parvati, my mother's mom, that is my Nani, like a pretty white flower, looked angelic. She was holy. She had been on her own since her husband died.

The partition of India and Pakistan in 1947 scarred all families on either side of the border. My Nana and Nani travelled as refugees in a police-guarded train coupe, along with their sons and daughters, to India.

THE TWO NANIS

Sadly, Nana died young, soon after he came to free India.

Nani's father rode the refugee train from Pakistan to India in the searing Indian summer during the riots of 1947, sitting on the roof of the train along with a thousand other exiles. He never quite recovered from the traumatic partition either, or regained his health. He too died in free India soon after.

My Nani turned to religion, her recourse, her solace, in times when spirituality was a natural progression. Interestingly, she was the daughter of a very high-thinking, and saintly man who never visited a temple or prayed.

Ramrakkhi Masiji, the visiting Nani, looked even more angelic than her sister Parvati, my Nani.

She was probably closer to the heavenly beings, always sensing she might be with them soon.

You see, her husband, Lala Devidas, had strangled his first wife on suspicion of being unfaithful.

He had just choked her with her own necklace, her gold chamkali, pulling the string around her neck tighter and tighter. So insanely jealous he became, when a mischievous rumor came to his ear, that she was looking down the balcony at a young man!

LALA DEVIDAS STRANGLING HIS WIFE WITH HER NECKLACE

She was innocent; she hadn't even looked; she let alone winked at a passing youth; she didn't have a lover; she was punished but blameless.

She died, and Lala Devidas spent time in jail.

And the second wife, Ramrakkhi, learnt piety.

The angels might protect her, and if they couldn't, she would go and be with them.

That is, in case the old man became insanely jealous again or very mad.

Her Delhi visits were thus a safe haven from her angry old man in Amritsar.

He remained angry quite often, though he was very loving when we children visited him.

Ramrakkhi Nani was an important guest here, fawned and doted upon.

Back home, probably a neglected old grandmother, always fearful of Lalaji's temper, she would stay in Delhi for a period and then, sadly, leave her sister to go back home.

Hours spent together praying and meditating in silent companionship with her dear sister, remembered by us, must surely have been a great solace and memory for her too.

I remember clearly my Nani, or Bhabij, as she was called. Tiny and fair, her head always a little unsteady in frailty, a stream of unspoken love pouring from her gaze.

Known for her gentle and sweet disposition, she had my fiery grandmother, Dai, my father's mother, in awe of her.

Rightly, Dai would say, the family was a family of 'devtas', or divine beings.

Halos, or glowing auras, are mere words.

But she was!

Bauji Ki Dhoti

Of all the Indian apparel, the strangest is the men's dhoti, 3 or 4 yards long, a wrap for men.

Bauji, the eldest of my three Mamajis, my maternal uncles, ie. mother's brothers, chose to wear a dhoti. Indeed, it was the dress of his time. A four metre saree-like wrap, tied at the waist and then divided between the legs for easy walking.

One hand held one end of the dhoti, low and stylishly. A marvel of draping!

Not imaginable, unless I tell you it was a bit like harem pants, but if unwrapped, just a length of fabric, a man's sari.

But worn, a garment; for the magic lay in the draping.

So suited to our climate, the flimsy light Mulmul cotton fabric was airy, and the draping ensured a lot of exposed hairy leg to keep men cool in tropical hot summer days. Hence, many old - timers resisted adopting trousers, the dress of their colonial British masters.

Not without its hazards, this garment was prone to wardrobe malfunctions. I mean, I always find it risky that it is held together with neither a pin nor a belt. Just tuck, fold, and tuck again. How?!

Doesn't the imagination boggle now?

Well, nothing ever happened to Bauji's dhoti, except on one unforgettable occasion.

Bauji was the least likely to adopt the newer western fashions. Most respectable, a sober, unruffled man, always perfectly turned out in crisp, starched white dhoti, a pristine white long kurta, gold buttons on the shirtfront, matching gold cufflinks, the fob watch, also gold, on a chain looping out of his breast pocket, and a black toupee, Nehru toupee, as it was known. He was elegant.

Till the fiasco of his eldest son's wedding.

Now, this eldest son, Krishan, was never to be married. An obstinate, wayward bachelor, not a single girl was good enough to be his bride. Not good-looking enough, not smart, or 'convent educated', no one ever measured up to his yardstick. For his life mate, he had created a paragon of virtues and beauty, an amalgam of all his past girlfriends.

He said, 'Bells should ring in my heart when I see her'.

So far, no music!

Then, lo and behold, one day he succumbed to the charms of a schoolteacher! A strict schoolmarm. No one asked about the ringing of the bells; the family was relieved he'd got over that obsession at the ripe age of 40 years.

Festivities broke out, and the joy in Nanighar, my grandmother's house, was infectious.

News spread that the eldest boy in the family was to be wed. Everyone knew.

As every Indian wedding brings, relatives came from far off, Kanpur and Amritsar, all housed at home.

The house itself was full of fun and bonhomie; cousins, friends, and relatives, all gathered for a few days, under one roof. Food galore, with the halwai, sweetmeat maker, making sweets and savouries, by the mountains, in the rear verandah. Endless coming and going.

Utter confusion prevailed. All young ones like us had taken off from schools and colleges to be merry-making, a holiday from boredom and routine.

Old aunts and uncles gossiped and revisited old quarrels, over tea and savoury mathis, with pickles.

The harassed mother and hostess had so much on her hands, no time to eat or chat.

Bauji, and all his younger brothers, the junior mamas shared responsibilities, supervising lights being put up, flowers on the wedding 'vedi or mandap', food arrangements, deliveries, tents being erected.

Noise, music, songs, chatter...

On the morning of the wedding, as is customary, Eunuchs turned up for a handout, to dance at the wedding and make some money and take something back, maybe 100, 200, or even 500 rupees. A whole bunch of them, six at least, luridly made-up, male bodies in feminine clothes, clapping and singing, likely to turn aggressive if not paid, determined to make something that day. Standing at the gate, demanding to see the boss of the household, anyone who held the purse strings.

At the very same time, a bandarwala, the monkey man, with his performing pair of monkeys dressed as bride and groom, found his way to the shaadi ghar, or wedding house. He was all set to put on a show and make a quick buck. He would enact a mock wedding. The kids got excited at the prospect of a show!

Two monkeys getting married, oh wow! Even better than the son getting married!!

A bandarwala is always fun for children; he always has a new show. No one thought of cruelty to animals, if any, in those days. So, with his noisy hand-held drum, or damru, the bandarwala made the monkeys, dressed as a bride and a groom, dance around each other. All of us in a circle, watched.

And just at the gate, the Eunuchs sang and danced, even though they were not welcome.

Loud and bawdy, dancing and clapping noisily with weird swaying movements, they were embarrassing to watch but could not be ignored. The monkeys, hearing the beat of the damru, became crazy and frisky, screeching and coming close to the half - scared, half - excited children. The two shows together and all the wedding activity was a heady, uncontrollable mixture, as only an Indian wedding can provide.

Bauji was not to be suckered into parting with money for these vulgarities. He began arguing with them, asking them to be off.

Do you think they'd leave?

Never!!

It was a celebration, and they would have their pound of flesh. The Eunuchs lifted their sarees intimidatingly and unashamedly, made rude gestures, getting obscener by the minute. The monkeys screeched louder than the damru, the hand-held drum. The situation got out of control.

Even neighbours, hearing this brouhaha, came running to watch the drama and tamasha.

Children, maamees, aunts, uncles, grandmothers, wedding guests, servants, neighbours, passersby, one and all.

The little naughty monkey plucked at Mamaji's dhoti, tugging and tugging, and ran off tearing it. The now, half torn dhoti was trailing on the floor. Mamaji could not fight him off.

Reddening, Mamaji cursed and shouted, raved and ranted, and finally shooed out the bandarwala and his monkeys. Palmed off a 100 rupee note into the hands of the grasping Eunuchs. And fled to his room with the half dhoti around him.

All the children, witnessing this unheard-of unravelling, were laughing mirthfully. Rolling on the ground, holding their stomachs, they said, "dhoti le gaya bandar, Bauji ki dhoti bandar le gaya," and "The monkey took away the dhoti." The Mamees laughed behind their saree pallus, the guests, and the servants all laughed, hiding their faces from Mamaji, the elder of the household. All the visitors marked this as the highlight of the wedding.

And it was etched in their memories forever and ever, and probably talked about at every subsequent wedding.

This hilarious incident was more fun than the 'bandar ka lagan', or even the wedding of Krishan.

Abudullah

I waited nervously below my apartment block. Waited for this man sent by the husband's office.

He was going to teach me to pass my driving test. I had been driving for years but there was no hope in hell of getting a driving license in this foreign country, Sharjah, an emirate of UAE, in the Middle East, so paranoid about giving freedom to women and foreigners.

All this in years gone by, in 1982 to be precise.

Yea, this was how it was in Dubai and Sharjah, neighbouring Emirates in the 1980s.

Women would constantly fail their driving tests. So would men. Having a fifteen-year-old driving licence from India didn't count.

The inspector was gleefully out to make you nervous and eventually fail you, everyone knew. I was understandably anxious.

My two little babies were in the secretary's care, sitting upstairs. And here I was waiting for Abdullah, reputed to be the instructor whose students passed, first shot.

A car drew up. The familiar office driver stopped, 'Salam, Begum Sahiba'.

He introduced me to the man I'd been waiting for.

Abdullah.

My eyes registered mild shock!

Abdullah was a huge broad giant, clad in Shalwar Kurta.

Dark, with a beehive beard, small black eyes that bored into you, lot of curly hair, Abdullah was a fearsome looking Pathan. He was familiar with the reaction he evoked.

'Begum Sahiba, hamaray chehray par mat jaaeyay. Hum jaisay lagtain hain, waisay hain nahin'.

'I am not as I look',he almost apologised, in his accent so novel to me.

He knew, could see my reaction, my apprehension.

I was hesitant of going out with him, alone in a car, in a strange land where I knew almost no one.

Recent entrant to the Middle East, I was still wary of everything.

This police state, with its strange laws, the military at the airport, high handed 'shurtas' or policemen, everywhere, was strangely restrictive. The daily freedoms we took for granted in India were under scrutiny.

I'm sure bare headed foreign women, driving, shopping, running about their daily lives freely, were a strange sight for them, in the land where their own women were cloistered. I was scared here.

Long working hours for the husband, I'd only see him by night.

I really would have to find my way about it. Nishant had to be admitted to school, driven for swimming lessons, my supermarket trips, Gautam, still a baby in arms, needed his inoculations......never ending tasks of a young mother!

I needed a car and I needed to drive to reclaim my mobility and my freedom. This burly, fierce looking man was going to be my passport to all that.

Feigning courage, I slipped into the driver's seat, next to him, and my lessons began. As did my falling under the spell of this rustic Afghan driver; he was like no one I'd ever met before.

'Begum Saahiba, aapko gaadi chalaana to aata hai, lekin tareeka sahi nahi hai'.' Aapko shurta fail kar degaa'.

You can drive, but not perfectly.

The policeman inspector would surely fail me, Abdullah was certain.

My driving skills did not impress him.

The training began.

Learning to reverse park a big car in a tight spot, between two four-wheel drives, parking at an incline and sitting hand free without sliding back, changing lanes safely, circumventing the narrow lanes of the bazar or 'souk'.... full of pedestrians and traffic, but mostly driving fast and confidently on their expressways.

I needed to learn all this and more.

A steady stream of conversation to keep me engaged and distracted. Abdullah, with his Afghani accent, was a superb talker.

Begum Sahiba, ' Pathan ki dosti mushoor hai, lekin iss se barr kar kya hota hai?'

What is even better known than a Pathan's friendship?

'Kya?' I was dumbfounded.

'Pathan ki dushmani'. His enemity!

Obvious. I should have known. Pathans are fiercely loyal as they are antagonistic.

'Aap ko malum hai, Pathan ke paas paisa aata hai to woh pehle cheez kya khareedta hai?'

What does a Pathan buy first when he has money?

Befuddled. 'Kya?'

Enormously proud, with chest swelling, to announce, 'Bundookh.' A gun!

'Kyon?' Incredulous, I had to ask why.

'Pathan ka dushman, uskay bhai ka bhi dushman, vo uski kaum ka bhi dushman samjaa jata hai'. 'Dushman se ladai ke liya Bundookh ka hona zaroori hai.'

A basic philosophy they lived by.

A Pathaan's enemy is his brother's enemy, his entire clan's enemy. To fight our enemies, we need guns.

Their loyalty to their family and community is legendary.

'Left ko park kariyay, '. I signalled, veering left to park.

'No Parking sign likhaa hai, chalaan hoga,'.

You will be challaned.

'Lekin aapnay kahaa....', but you said.... I trailed off...

'Aapko dekh ke park karna hai'. See signage before you park.

Teaching me how my driving test inspector would try to confuse me, he was aware of their tricks.

'Pathan ko sabse pyaaraa kya hota hai?' What does a Pathan love the most?

'Kya?' I asked.

'Watan', his homeland, he said with a faraway look.

Strains of the famous song from the film 'Kabuliwala', echoed in my mind. 'Ae meray pyaaraaa watan......Ae meray bichray chaman...'. One of my favourites.

My distant beloved homeland.........

The Kaabuliwala from Kabul, who was a merchant in a faraway land sang, sang nostalgically to a little girl, when she reminded him of his daughter, left back home. A Pathan misses his beloved rugged country, his home and family, he can never detach from.

'Left lijeeyay, '. A No Entry sign in the narrow lanes of the old souk, hardly prominent amid the hustle and bustle, the crowds, winked at me.

'No Entry hai ',I caught his trickery this time. He was trying to distract me with conversation, so I would forget the rules.

'Shabaash, shurtaa (police inspector) aiyse he aapko galati karaayay gaa, aur phir fail karegaa'. This is how the inspector would try to trick me, and fail me.

We drove up a hill in the practice area. Right at the incline, 'gaadi rokiyay'.

I braked on the pedal and stopped; the car rolled back.

'Fail. Handbrake laggaiyay'.

Standstill.

The burly black bear smiled, his eyes twinkled, no longer mean.

And I was no longer afraid. A human bond had been forged.

My second lesson the next day was learning how to drive, maintaining a fast, even speed, on the highway. I'd never driven so fast back home; our roads are too crowded.

Abdullah wished me luck for my driving test. I watched him go, this garrulous, very open Afghan man, insightful for me, warm in his fashion; both of us foreigners in a country reluctant to offer friendship, or let you into their homes, their culture and their ways.

I've always found ordinary people in their simple ways the most interesting. I've never forgotten Abdullah, my driving instructor.

And I passed my driving test first shot. And the inspector did ask me to turn into a 'No Entry' lane, but I was ready.

The Matriarch

On the Emirates flight from NYC to Dubai

My husband always finds much to laugh at about my family; we are a constant source of mirth to him. Our eccentricities only became apparent to me, it seems, after they were first noticed by him, almost right after the day I got married, lying dormant all my previous life.

It's the perspective, so to say. Now, I never had it. I mean, this vision of clarity regarding my family.

Or even his family, for that matter. Probably because, till I got married, I never had in-laws.

At least that sounds logical.

Not that strange things were not happening right under my unsuspecting newlywed nose. They were.

But the young nose was a little gullible and innocent then, olfactorily deficient, so to say.

Right at the time I got married, my in-laws lived in Goa.

All, two sisters-in-law, married and unmarried, brother-in-law, father-in-law, and a fresh little in-law, a yowling, howling brat, six months into the job.

She's now a Vice President or a President, of a foreign company based in Singapore, but at the time, I would not have suspected she'd be more than a howler. Unbelievable!

And, of course, most importantly, my Mother-in-Law.

The house on the beach, set amidst tall, swaying palms, not far from the sun drenched sea, was idyllic.

Not romantically, however.

I was the new entrant into the great Indian family, the novice to be inducted into their superior ways. Stolen glances at my husband were always intercepted. Never by him however; I wonder why.

I had no choice but to get to know them, was my brief, soldierly speaking.

I did too!

At night, the wind howled and whistled through the swaying palms, rustling through the entire house, whispering delightedly to the trees, the doors and windows, and everything else, 'Oh, it's coming, the monsoon is coming. It's coming!'

The season most longed for, for its drenching, quenching rains!

And here by the sea, most eerie too, outdoors at night, amid rustling, swishing, hissing palms, casting strange shadows, the monsoon was awaited.

The Matriarch Rama Malhotra

One such squally, windy night, I awoke to find everyone awake. Bit confused and mortified that I had overslept, an absolute no-no, not done, by the new daughter-in-law, in the big joint family of then.

But it turned out that we might have an intruder. Yes, my mother-in-law had heard scary sounds and woken up my father-in-law, who was now on the job, checking the house from outside to in, cupboard to drawer, balcony to ledge.

It can't be done without waking up everyone, including the newlyweds. Dutifully, one joined the search.

Nothing and no one was found.

'But I definitely heard a door creaking and something dropping', Ma -in-law firmly told bleary-eyed Pa-in-law.

More looking under the beds now and under carpets too. The robber must now be very scared. What a diligent search party, commandeered by such a stately Matriarch!

An hour into the search, tea was made to calm Mother's frayed nerves.

The others wanted it too, so dutifully, another pot was boiled.

Not to be outdone, wanting her pound of flesh, the smallest in-law, Sonu, six months old, now joined the search for the petrified robber, who might have been shivering under the bed, had he really been there.

Back then, I did not know.

The littlest investigator did this with a piercing howl, wanting its share of action. Freshly diapered soon. Big sister-in-law Punam, made a bottle of milk for this noisy infant, others scurrying, still looking for the absent thief.

Finally, big brother-in-law Goga, annoyedly declared that there was no thief and that mummy had woken up everyone for nothing. Not to be put down, she said she had definitely heard something.

But she was now calm, tea in hand, the infant being fed on her bed, daughter-in-law, that is me, carrying the tea tray to the others.

Bahadur, the watchman, at the gate now on guard duty instead of slumbering, and most of all, my father-in-law not snoring now.

She'd managed to stop that awful noise at last. She was happy.

A Matriarch in her mettle, the whole house revolving around her. Bustle and hustle in a house awake at 3 a.m.! Not tossing about through her sleeplessness.

At that time, I did not know. She was a terrible insomniac, sleeping beside an oblivious railway

SOM DUTT MALHOTRA MY FATHER-IN-LAW

station, my father-in-law, snoring like whistling trains all night, night after night.

I don't know if he saw through her ruse, my poor father-in-law.

She'd think of another one if he got too much again.

But all the family finally did, quite soon!

And the railway station became my lot too.

I have a whole railyard to sleep alongside. The husband whistles all night.

Genetics, they call it!

Bade Chor

One marries, arranged as it often is, here in India, as mine was, full of trepidation.

The nervous young girl worries.

One has high expectations. But surprises await.....

Fresh into Malhotra clan, my new family, married ten days in all, we did a car trip to Vengurla. Vengurla is not too far from Goa, where the family stayed.

The car was packed with mother-in-law, two sisters-in-law, Punam and Bubli, a small wee brat Sonu, husband Naresh, brother-in-law Sudesh, and my father-ln-law.

Eight stuffed one atop the other in an Ambassador car.

Vengurla was where the ever-so-delicious famed Mankuri mango, grew.

I didn't know then that the Malhotras were besotted with the rich yellow fruit and would go to any lengths for it.

The month was May, the mango season, when large tempting green mangoes are beckoning from the trees.

In another few days they would turn yellow and sweet and ready to be harvested.

But we were here today, so the crime had to be committed here and now.

Being the only outsider, a new entrant into the family, this was my first experience of a marauding, thieving clan to which I now belonged.

The car was brought to a silent halt. As if by some unspoken understanding, all jumped out and crept along the wall of the mango grove. No one in sight, Punam nimbly climbed up, Naresh pointing out the largest mangoes, Bubli to catch the mangoes that were plucked and Punam threw.

Lightning fast, a raid of stealth was conducted, several low and high hanging mangoes plucked with magnificent speed. And we sped away!

Yours truly was heart-thumpingly astound, never having been part of a mango raiding party before. The (vegetarian) chicken in me expected to be apprehended anytime, even though I never plucked even a single mango, refusing to come down from my high moral ground.

AAM KI CHORI

I learnt later they all had a twisted upbringing. The two brothers and their sister were regularly confined to the bathtub, in the mango season in, clad in just 'chaddis', a huge basket of mangoes between them to gorge. When they were done, they washed up. With tummies bulging, happy faces, no need for dinner, they went about their business.

The mango season brought such delicious longings for the king of fruits, the Malhotras could even rob for them. It's hard to erase such torturous memories.

Years rolled by, with grey hair and age, now all commanded much respect. The brothers were heads of companies; well known, pillars of society.

Sisters -in -law had children to be raised with values and ethics.

Petty crime was behind them.

But the past has a way of popping up again in the strangest of ways. And years later.....

Just the other day, I noticed our neighbour's mango tree laden with fruit, high, but large and green, and begging to be assaulted. Our tree in contrast, bore no flower or fruit that year.

It saddened my husband, reminded of our last year's bounty, when we harvested massive sized Malligae mangoes with a wonderful fragrance and juicy yellow fruit.

The effect of the neighbor's tree on hubby made the years roll by. I was the same newly wedded girl in love with my man. He had the same look of lust in his eyes. His jaw slackened and he licked his chops.

But it was for the mangoes, not his wife. I knew his intent instinctively.

I hadn't been married to him for so long for nothing.

I was horrified, this was Chinky's, a neighbour and friend's tree, not just some unknown wayside farm. I argued to no avail.

A gleeful, conniving bunch of minions was assembled.

In no time the climbing human monkeys had harvested huge baskets of mangoes.

Cooks and cleaners, watchmen too, all became mango robbers.

"Fruit hanging on our side of the wall belongs to us, rightfully, and legally, no arguments", I was educated.

Husband's word is law in my house.

Mortified that my neighbour would chide us, I scolded all the colluders, only to be told,

"Woh memsaab bahar hain, kya bhi malum nahin parta".

'The memsaab is not here, she'll never know'.

'Hun ki karnaa' ? What to do now?

If you can't beat them, join them.

Within minutes saunf, kalongee, mirchi, methi, salt, mustard oil and other special ingredients were procured. All the evidence had to be obliterated.

So we chopped, pickled, chutneyed and concealed it in jars. Now the jars are sitting in the sun; who is to tell whose mangoes they they were.

Arrogantly and proudly husband surveyed the lined up pickled parade.

But I had crimes in my family to be proud of too.

My grandfather's brother Lala Devidas strangled his very beautiful first wife with her own necklace. She, he suspected, was carrying on with another. So jealous was he!

What a crime of passion! In hushed tones it was whispered, with some pride, forever after.

He was jailed. His eldest brother Rai Bahadur Jessaram went to plead with the Commissioner of Police for leniency. He was also put behind bars, even though he had been conferred the title of 'Rai Bahadur', by the British, in Dera Ismail Khan.

But that was my illustrious family!

Here in my new Malhotra family the level of crime was a bit low.

Chori? For mangoes? Just mangoes?!!

Murder is a bit beyond their capabilities.

The great grandchildren of ours, my grandchildren's children will be able to say with pride, "bade Dadaji aam ke chor thay. Bade Chor".

My Malhotra family, I think, they don't see straight when they see mangoes.

For them, mangoes are to die for, my family will tell you. Or live for!

Especially stolen mangoes!! Nothing sweeter than stolen mangoes!!!

Of Brooms Mice And Dragons

Morning, or early morning, is a state of innocence. So are we, with our nightclothes askew, hairdo tangled, pointy, or witchy.

I watched, propped up on three pillows, a blob of foam left under the nose of the shaving husband. My slow right eye still wandering, not having returned to focus from the night's nightmares.

One is not quite ready yet to face the world.

We had yet to fix our smiles and our minds to face the day.

And then, what does one say to one bucket and broom that glides past the Saab and Memsaab in their bedrooms to go across to the balcony with so much businesslike haste.

The young, purposeful owner of the cleaning equipment has an urgent job to do and can't be stopped.

I mused, thinking that I had said, ' Baad mein', meaning 'later', some days ago.

I repeated, Baad mein', abhi Saab ready hota, office jaana hai. Saab has to go to office.

Baad mein aana.'

Deference.

The smiling one withdrew, and we got back our privacy to shave and get on with other unmentionables, fixing ourselves for the day, you know, like the missing eyebrow, hearing aids, nostril hair, and such. The denture stage is not yet here.

Can't get more personal than that.

Just five minutes later…

From the corner of my eye, I behold someone in the planter box of the first floor guest bedroom, actually standing in the planter box, visible from my bedroom.

The box is just a foot wide, externally protruding from the wall, empty because we removed the plants, and accessible only if you walk the plank, or rather the sunshade. Now, whence did this brat get there, and why?!

This cleaning maniac, the boon of my home and bane of my privacy, was out there, singing some forest people's songs and rhythmically moving the duster, left to right, right to left.

I screeched for her safety. She turned and grinned happily, having got a surface to play with but not being able to hear me through the glass.

I looked at the happy person so far from her own home, such sunshine in mine.

This was my forest tribal girl, Bala, whom I love because she is, as a human should be, a great doer and giver.

What could I have given this one beyond money? Not a fraction of what I received.

In the course of the day, when I found myself home from my wanderings, on top of my job list, dry cleaning retrieved, subzi, and beer having been acquired, I noticed my small mouse in the garden.

Freshly recruited this new, fresh, pink offspring of some bigger mouse was masquerading as my watchman. He held a stick over his head and was shouting to keep the squirrels away from my 'anaars', or pomegranates. Now the squirrels were larger and could have eaten him rather than the raw annars.

He decidedly looked juicier, but the squirrels were fooled by his disguise, looking like a biggish human, when actually he was a little pink mouse, with a thatch of light hair and a worried, earnest expression.

His task was tough, guarding the fruit and keeping the garden spruce.

He took his job seriously.

The squirrels were denied their delight by the mouse dressed as a human.

He is actually the father of two little pink mice. I wonder what his lady mouse looks like!

This year, the tree yielded more than sixty big, beautiful anaars. Last year, the squirrels must have feasted on many more.

Why was the mouse saving fruit from squirrels for an ogre, the Memsaab, who lived in the house?

Like my forest girl, he is an enigma to me.

But I have a Dragon too. I have locked up a Dragon in my dungeon for the past 25 years. Actually, the Dragon is my keeper, and I am at it's mercy.

This place belongs to it. The Dragon guards it jealousy, snorting and blowing plumes of fire and smoke regularly. Sometimes they singe me.

No one can escape its wrath.

Not Bibi, that's me, not the minions like the brown mouse masquerading as a watchman, or the tribal forest girl, or any others. No one can escape its fearsome blaze.

The Dragon is always watching, eagle-eyed, giving orders to all dreamers and the lazy Memsaab.

'Ye laao, vo karo, usko phone karo, medicine ka goli khaao, Saab ka beer laao, watchman ko gussa karo, maali masti karta hai'........

It's a non-stop assault on my senses, which want to remain senseless.

But I love my Dragon. It became my mother. The angel, who was mom, went to meet God and left a Dragon to watch over all of us, the shaving husband and the two wicked offspring.

It's now hounding the sleepy slob Boochie, my lazy fat cat, to take her evening constitutional in the garden.

'Sair karo, moti nahin hona, dactur bola'.

No one can escape my Dragon.

Not even Booch, the 'Sher ki Masi', our beloved cat.

I wonder, is the Dragon afraid of anyone? Who is its keeper?

Sher Ki Masi – 1

Boochspeak

2015

I'm a bus stop cat. No, a railway station cat; maybe a cat from the park?

They can't make up their minds about where they found me.

But I was found. Found by the maali, Aslam the gardener. He brought me here cupped in his hands, all the way from wherever.

I was so happy. Because where I was found was so noisy, it was crazy; everything around me was zooming, and huge creatures were stomping all over the place. I was afraid, hiding in a corner.

I'd lost my mama. And all my brothers and sisters.

So that's how Aslam found me.

I was an orphan; but I had a whole other family with me. They all came with me. Hidden in my fur, in my head, in my tummy, in my armpits. Lots of friends, running all over. But they were very, very naughty, running all the time in my fur and making me scratch. It's not nice to race all over someone's head; quite confusing, in fact!

So, they had to be thrown out.

Aslam gave me to the girl who gives me food. She's, my keeper. I hate it when she's not there.

If she's there, then I don't mind who comes or goes. Her name is Hajji.

She gave me to the big boy Nish, who became my papa. He put me in his pocket, where I fitted perfectly. With my entire family.

I fell asleep. I think all my small friends also fell asleep. We were so cosy. I like to sleep on him. I still do, even though I'm a big girl now.

Whenever he's around, I find him and sleep on his big front. For hours.

He loves me, my favourite, and I his.

They called me Boochie. I can guess why. It's because, I think, I came with a lot of Boochies from the noisy bus stop.

My friends, you see, were all boochies, insects, fleas, ticks.

But my keeper shouts a lot. Starts shouting from early morning when she lets me out. Always cornering me, even when I go for my morning fitness.

'Heh, heh, heh', she heckles as she marches me in a straight line.

Cats don't walk in a straight line, you ignoramus.

A cat needs to sharpen her claws, run about to keep speed, and catch some rats. Have some self-respect.

But this one is always in my face, too queasy or what, she won't let me catch my food!

Her food is so yukk, inedible!

Always screeching. Screeching in the garden, when I find a catch, chance upon a slithery lizard or roach, yelling even if I get inside the plates cupboard or the laundry, always screeching. It's so annoying!

Hey! I like to be among clothes in the cupboards. I love laundry. And I love slapping lizards.

She's only happy if I'm toasting myself on the hot box, that transformer, on top of the fridge.

So, she can watch me all the time! Policing!

But I like to hide; I like to explore. It's a big house, with so many nooks and perches, I'm so fond of.

The top of the cupboards is so safe, and all mine.

No one can get me. I can see what they're up to, but they don't know where I am.

Sometimes I find a higher ledge in the box room. I burrow and fall asleep so nicely. It's warm and so safe, behind the big boxes, hidden from all. Once, I think I got locked in the store. For many, many hours. They forgot me. It was delightful.

I could hear them shouting about me downstairs, fighting about who lost me, who left the door open.

But do you think they'll let me be? Come hunting and calling my name, peering here and there, unlocking doors, even going to the backyard, all over the garden, disturbing me.

"Boochie, Musu, Poochie, where are you? " Gets my goat.

And when they find me, boy, I get scolded again for being a naughty cat. I'm afraid they'll never figure it out. I like to be naughty.

I love being lost, not found and shamed.

The top of the cupboard is just the very best. Right amid the old newspapers, my own fur, and my own smells.

You see, they don't sweep it every day; it's mine. I don't have to share it with anyone. I've even peed there.

Long ago. On the tennis racquet. That other boy's, who comes sometimes, on whose cupboard I sleep.

And when I get up there, I won't come down till you make me. I just won't.

Come on, make me, make me; first get my claws, and then get my treats, yummy, yummy ones.

They are very mingy and stingy about my treats.

I have to work for them; otherwise, I'll never get them. The other boy, they call Gautam, brings the treats from far away.

It's his room. He lets me bleed his hand and chew it. He's the doctor.

They put my treats on the ground, so I have to jump down to get them. And sadly be pounced upon.

Thank God I don't have to share my treats with my keeper, who gives me food.

One day, I was snoozing upstairs in a sunny spot. No one up there.

Oh, it was so heavenly!

My ears pricked. I heard a bell, an unfamiliar sound, and a new smell. Someone new was inside and was making his way up. I didn't like it.

It was a big person, carrying a box.

I scampered up the cupboard.

I saw he carried a big ladder, my ladder, which is always in my sleep room at night.

I go up and I go down my ladder all night, just checking. I love ladders, but he climbed my ladder and started poking things.

Now it's my house, I don't like new people coming to look at me, pretending to touch the fans, the lights, and the windows.

They stare at me, and I stare right back, not afraid. Let them try something; I'll show them. I've got my claws ready. Intruders!

They do this all the time. New people with bags and boxes; new cleaning girls; big people poking taps and lights. They all come to disturb me in my house. I don't go to theirs.

I'd like to see what's inside their boxes and bags.

Some of the girls are okay. One cleans my water bowl. Another left the window open. I jumped out onto the sunshade. Wow! You know. I've been to the terrace. It's so high, they plucked me back.

The last one used to leave the back door open all the time; she was the best. I could run into the garden and chase butterflies; no one the wiser.

The girls leave me alone.

Know I will scratch.

BOOCHIE - SHER KI MASI

The garden is my haven. Eventually, of course, they have to come and get me. They don't feel happy without locking me in. Jailers!

I'm their Boochie Boo, they say! Whatever!

Jailers, Killjoys.....Keeepers!

Sher Ki Masi – 2

'**M**y Furball!'

No room for anything but breathless, mushy, overflowing emotion.

All for my small, small ball of fur.

'Striped and spotted, long and deep-haired, what thick and beautiful fur!' breathlessly spoken.

Dare you touch it; fur goes left or right in a smooth silken wave.

Dare to rumple it; it grrrgrowls.

Stroke it under the chin or behind the ears; it purrs in ecstasy. 'Rrrrrrrrrrrrrr'

But fall in love with the tiger spots on the stomach and let your hand stray.....it becomes a warning growl. 'Hissssssss', I'm a cat snake.

It's confusing. I'm confused. Never heard any other cat hiss.

My, my, my interactive furball soft toy.

Warm. And soft. Evokes violent desires, squashing, and mauling. Kissing. All animal desires, as animal as my little animal, Bussu Furball.

Furru has a long day. It wakes up after a bad night.

I would say generally every night must be bad for this little miss.

She's a night insomniac. Watchman on a watch.

And a lazy, sleepy puss all day. Sleeps the day away.

Early morning, she hammers the garage door, kickboxing, to be let out.

Sometimes drumming away for a longish time. Bang bang...bang bang.... bang.

When opened, the garage shows all the debris of war, a one-girl war, or one Bushu war of fighting with the upturned mattress, ripping newspapers from cover to cover, like a lil' wolverine. Overturning the sand tray and the water bowl. Probably mixing to make sandcastles? All topsy-turvy!

Chasing imaginary mice all night.

Out now, in the garden for her morning's graze. Tiny bits of grass. Now she's a lil' cow!

Eats grass every day. Chomp, chomp. Tasty grass, she moves from the shade grass to the Korean. She has her day's preferences.

Sated, she lies now under a bush or shady tree, surveying the creatures big and small. The day's delights.

Overhead, a crow gets her attention. Assesses. Vile thing is too high. Abort attempt.

Rigid now with excitement, as a butterfly flits past. She runs and jumps up to grab it.

It flutters past her very nose, teasing. Missed!

Flopped down after her failed attempt and vexed, claws retracted, watching fixedly.

Next instant, mouthwateringly, a dragonfly zooms across.

Crow, butterfly, and then dragonfly.

Glazed and confused. Yet another desired victim, but all missed.

Nothing, nothing, nothing caught, not a thing. Bah!

What's a girl to do? The garden is a pitfall of attractions.

And fat Boochie can't leap high enough.

Miss Predator, frustrated with no kill, ran her fat self up a tree, quickly sharpened her claws and then shamefully fell down. Plonk!

Ignominious for an arrogant 'Sher ki Masi', lion's aunt.

By which time, 'Saab ke nashta dena hai', breakfast to be given to the boss, she was unceremoniously scooped up by her morning walker, and deposited indoors, the main door firmly shut; her hopes dashed to the ground.

Butterflies and dragonflies, crows and sparrows, flying morsels and playmates, all locked outside, under the blue sky, on a breezy morning, and I am here?

Hrumph!

Babe sulks near the sunny spot by the French windows. Wrapped like a samosa or an Egyptian mummy, front paws crossed over, head between paws, eyes accusing.

Where's my papa? I want to poke poke his front.

Saab meanwhile is having breakfast. Ready to go out soon.

Hey, maybe I can go along, reasons our little miss.

Hopeful, Bushu parks herself near the main door, staring straight ahead, into the teak wood. I might be able to slip through the crack, she thinks.

'Not today, not now!'. Says another voice.

Thrown back again into the house.

Human killjoys!

Everyone is not around. Bushu suddenly finds her joy.

She scoots and chases and gets it, whoa, and goes wack, wack, and gotcha!

And then suddenly they are all over her, secret police, all of them.

Screams of disgust. 'Hai hai! Dirty girl! Throw it, throw it!

'Beebee Beebee'. Hajji is shouting to me.

'Dekho, dekho, dhar ek tarf, mundi ek tarf, chipluck ke do tukray karke, kaisa naach rahi hai, jallad',

'Chorungee nahi, bolti, kaisee hai yeh jaahil awlad?'.

She's playing with a dismembered lizard's writhing tail.

Wack, wack, wack, and another wack! With her tiny white, socked paws.

Dancing all around it, what a bizarre sight! But she loves it.

The frightened head of the lizard must have scampered away to safety to regrow.

Suddenly all pounce on Bushu. To prise her catch away.

She's cornered; she's miffed. Why? Why? Oh why? She sulks. You didn't find it. I did. It was mine.

You took away my toy.

Where's my papa? I was to poke poke his boob.

Booch has to make do with dry, tasteless cat food, that too KD, or kidney diet for adult cats.

What! Do adult cats have no taste buds? It's horrible.

She eats it all, all, and pushes her tray away in disgust.

Disdainfully walks away upstairs, in a peeve, to find herself a cosy place to get away from all.

The black bird, flirty butterfly, and my wriggly tail, all gone.......Life is so bad.

I'm going to bed.

Now what would be today's snooze spot?

The red sofa? Na. I did that yesterday.

The MD's chair? Yes, a favourite; it's at the top of my hidey hideouts list.

What about the fresh laundry? Nice soft white shirt? Let's snuggle in before they find me.

I'm so tired. Yawn yaaawwwn, a wide open yawn showing teeth to palate, ENT mysteries unfolded.

Where's my Pa...............pa.... I.....

Mmmmmm, deeper and deeper. Mmmmmm..........lost ....zzzz...

Actually snoring. Have you ever heard a cat snore? Like a small baby.

It's hilarious.

Her day is spent in delicious slumber, curled up like a prawn, in a sunny spot.

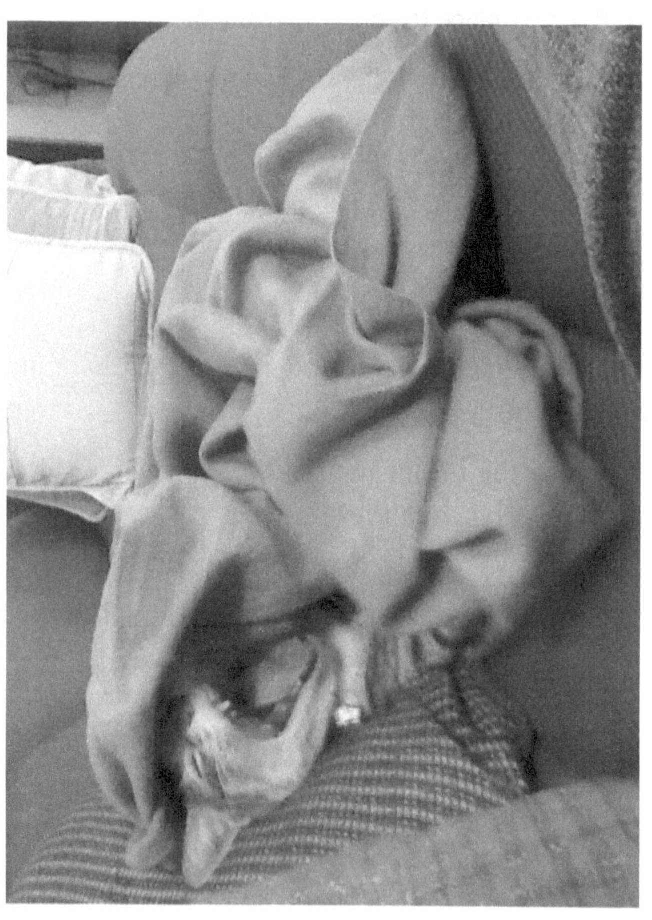

In Delicious Slumber

Oh, you jealous human monsters, you wish you could, as I do.

But... Where's my papa? I want to poke poke his boob.

Upside down, legs up in the air, slack mouth, frozen in a strange, twisted posture, Booshu is oblivious to the world, safe and secure on the soft shawl, on her papa's bed.

Lost to us all, for the time being.

(Boochie passed away on Sept.20th, 2024).

Chipluck

First drafted soon after spoken by our agitated cook, Hajji, in Hyderabadi Hindi, upon spying Boochie cat's dismembered victim. Screeched Hajji ....

Bibi, Bibi

Dhar ek tarf, mundi ek tarf, nach rahi, nach rahi

alag ja raha mundi, dabbay ke peechay chupney

Poonch hamki billi se jhagar rahi

De tamacha, de tamacha, usko de tamacha,

Aur phir, hamki billi nach nach kar, uskay upar phir rahi

Aagu bhi, peechu bhi, phir rahi,

uski kya haalath kari,

haibath aati hai,

Baba re baba,

kya bolun, bolnay ko nahin hota

Aisee aulad hai, jaahil,

chipluck ke do tukray karke bhi

khush nahin.

Aulad hai ke janwar?

Dhar: body

Mundi: head

Tamacha: slap

Nach: dance

Haibath: worry, panic

Chipluck: lizard

Aulad: offspring

Dadi Ki Shawl Mein

On a wintry evening a few years ago, around the time Chennai was experiencing a cyclone, it became very cold. Booch found the woollens cupboard open and snuck in to burrow into Dadi's, my mother in law's, shawl.

Thereafter, she just appropriated it. She still nuzzles into the warm shawl, years later, now meshed with her hair.

Barraa mazaa aa rahaa hai, Dadi ki shawl mein

Meri bhi vo dadi thi
Uski hi mein poti thi
Uska mera rishta thaa
Puranaa lambaa kissa tha.
Haqq to mera be kuch hoga
Shawl
meray he hissay mein aati thi
Kyon ki vo meri dadi thi.

Pota, poti, betaa, beti
Rishtaa sabhi batatay hain
Naata jorr, sabhi
ainth bahut dikhlaatay hain

BOOCHIE

MERI DADI, MERI SHAWL

Dekho, zoraa zori
mat karna
Varna, mazaa tumhay
Chakhaateen hoon

Cheen ke dekho
Shawl tum meri
Kya haal tumhara
Banati hoon

Char tango wali hoon
Sher ki mein Masi hoon
Shastr meray, daant aur nakhun
Khoon tumhara bahati hoon

Shawl par meraa he haqq hai
Baalon se mainay jarr le hai
Tumharay kaam na aati ab
Lapait ke mai soh jaati hoon

ainth: superiority
Shastr: weapons
haqq: ownership
jarr: meshed, decorated,
baalon: hair
Lapait: wrapped
Soh: sleep

Sapne Mein Aakar Dadi Boli

A reply to Dadi ki Shawl Mein

On her birthday March 27th, it was strangely wintry in 2016. Quite upset at the condition of her woollen shawl now ripped and matted with cat hair, at the hands or rather claws of Boochie, Dadi now extremely annoyed, exclaimed in Punjabi:

Dekh dekh ke sarrdhee haan
Shawl meri tu pandi hain
Main koi shawl ne ditti tennu
Jhootiyaan galla banandee hain

Kutti runn,
Tu ne koi poti shoti
Moti billo, phaj ja ethon
Katan teri boti shoti

Khoon tu meray bhachyaan da, vahandee hain
Khurundra maar, nakhoon saanu dekhandi hain ?
Jithay dekho, vaal hai teray
Gandh baraa machandi hain.

Koi ni tannu shawl mein dayni
Hadda fur coat tu pandi hain

Chuay khaani, kasmanu khaani
haddi pooch latkani hai

Nas ja ethon, moti billo
Hore kisay nu de deva gee.
Vaddi aayee meri poti shoti
Khoti mainu banannee hain?

Titli

BUTTERFLY

Boochie cat in the big garden, lusting after Titli.
It flits, it flies
It zooms, it glides
Almost glows in the sunlight
Before my very eyes.

It flutters
its blue wings
Flirty minx
This Butterfly.

I watch, I pray, I curse
It may fall down
on its own
In agony, I moan

I'm absolutely rapt
She's a butterfly
and I.,...
I am a cat.

I leap, I fall
I run, I stalk,
I have her now, and now...
Now she's gone

She's such a tease
A wretch, if you please.
She's the prey, I'm the hunter
She's the victim; I'm the master

But is it really so? Is it?
She just........ flies away
I look
Longingly hereafter.

She floats on the horizon
Quivering with the breeze
Kissing flower
Skimming with bees

I, grounded and earthed
With grass beneath my feet
I'm housed; she's free
I'm not even allowed a tree.

It is not so simple.....this equation
Of hunter and hunted
Of flyers and chasers
Victim and prey.

Am I one........ or the other?
Or is it
just the game
that I'm after?

How I Met Your Mother

FOR NIRVAAN

Panjim airport in Goa was very small in 1977. Only a few planes landed here.

When my husband and I got off the aircraft that March, it was very hot. I was to be met by my new family, the Malhotra family.

A new daughter-in -law going to be with her new family.

A little bundle had come to the airport along with them. It was all wrapped up. A small cap sat atop the bundle in the basket.

Was it laundry? Was it goodies? It could be anything; I was curious.

Could it be a puppy or a cat? Surely it was too large to be a mouse.? Mangoes?

Oh, what could be inside that bundle?!

I was dying of curiosity.

Suddenly, a piercing scream emanated from it. Much wiggling, and then tiny arms and legs kicked themselves out of the bundle!

Ooooo! It was a baby!

I lifted the cap to find a small, round face howling, but no tears. Just shamming. Horrid thing!

Round face, a button nose but huge eyes, and a big mouth. Boy, this one could make such a ballyhoo!

And whenever she was hungry, that was her way of telling us.

That was my introduction to Sonali, the newborn, your mother, just five months old, and come to welcome me into the family.

She was very cute, and she knew it. Wicked thing. She had us all in her spell in no time.

Baby Chipkali

L ost in no.1101 Malibu Town
A poor thing with a tail.

August 2, 2018

I'm lost. And I'm alone.

My Mummy and Daddy are big crawlies. They lost me. I can't even go up a wall.

I'm locked inside a big house in a bathroom. It's my jail.

No one ever comes to see me. Not even to say hello or put the lights on.

Nowadays one big fat old lady has come. She comes to the bathroom a lot, puts on the lights and makes lots of noise. They call her Chachi.

Every morning this nasty lady opens the water from the shower. I get so frightened because the water wets me. My wet feet won't crawl.

I lie in the corner and weep. But the mean old lady keeps on singing in the bath.

After many hours I dry out.

I'M WET

This morning the fat monster surprisingly became kind. She slid me on a piece of paper and set me down on the balcony.

I'm so happy I'm free and dry now. I'll grow big and strong and climb walls soon.

Then I'll have babies. But I'll never lose them in nasty places like bathrooms.

I Do Not Want to Write About

February 23, 2017

For Goga, when you were sick and we lost you in Max Hospital in Delhi.

I do not want
to write about
This place
I'm about.

Humans I see in pain,
dehumanised bodies in bed
with machines beeping
above their heads.

With masks and tubes
wires and metres
Surrounded by nurses and doctors
Technicians and catheters

Hovering around,
Beings, who may not want to be
Desperate, doubting, another day
They may, or may not see.

Sometimes in MRI, or X-ray,
Scanned, poked, prodded
Wheeled in and out,
Examined throughout.

I do not want
To write about
this place
I'm about.

Wrings my heart to see sick babies
In mother's arms cradled,
Following them, old grandfathers
Fretting and worried, themselves disabled.

Youths in wheelchairs
Hairless after chemo
Wan and hollow-eyed, hoping
For an end to their nightmares.

Afghans, Kashmiris
have travelled from far
Countrymen and foreigners
All the way from Africa.

It's teeming with the sick
Looking for succour
From trauma and cancer
That in this fearful age occur.

It pains my heart,
I do not want
to write about this place
I'm about.

Its memories will never fade
I'm afraid, one will be back
with another loved one,
At some future date.
And then..........In the cafeteria

The caregivers gorging on samosas
Between visiting hours
Drowning their worries
In sambhar and dosas.

Of waiting rooms
With chargers plugged
People talking and sharing stories.
Your father, my husband...details gory

Though I see suffering and pain
Happy and healed, many go home.
Sad days forgotten
To live again.

Others go with hope in the offing
Back to their hearths
Cared for, their suffering eased
Of their pain at least, released.

Many must go to their Master
Find their heavenly home hereafter
Their families bereaved
Of their dear ones relieved.

Constantly invoked
Of every faith
The gods themselves
Must dwell in this place.

This Max

I do not want to write about
This city of pain and hope
The sick
cannot do without

For when, Lord
You make us suffer a lot
Some we can bear
but some we cannot

Our anguish is all we can think about
Doctor doctor, healer, healer, come to me
Cure me, ease me
Relieve me

Max Max, this city of pain
Of hope and gain
Is a microcosm
Of our world without.

Winning and losing
But, oh, so intense
Life unfolded
Sometimes it doesn't make sense.

It's His will
The philosopher proclaims
Understanding nothing
Accepting the bill

Of money,
of joy, or pain
Of his loss
or gain

Max Max, o Max, o Max

I do not want
To write about

But please be there
When I need you

With your healers and nurses
Your cold, warm heart
Of mounting bills
But medicine, State of Art.

Max, Max, o Max, o Max.

My Dear Wall

July 2, 2019

When Miru was made to stand in a corner by her Mom, Ginkle, for some misdemeanor, a punishment she could not tolerate.

My dear Wall
I'm into you.
Booo hooo hoo
Can you help me please?
Tell my mom
To come
Hold me tight
With all her might
Say she's sorry
And tell me
She loves me
She'll do my bidding
For I'm no pudding
She thinks she knows
But she's a bully
I have a mind
Of my own
I want my way

MIRU IN THE WALL

Do this, do that
Away,
I want my way
Oh Wall
Please call
My mother
No other
To hold me tight
With all her might
And kiss my sobs
Away
Boo hoo hoo.
Oh Wall
I'm so small
So what?
All the time
I want my way
My way.

The Two of You

To the Sunflowers, Daises, Poppies, Tulips and the many adoring others.

November 2018

I see you looking at him all the time
And he too
looking and looking
A steady gaze,
What is between the two of you?

Your rapturous face upturned
Your being aglow, colour-suffused,
I see you turn towards him all the time
He too showers himself upon you,

What is between the two of you?

Arraigned in red, yellow, purple, and pink
You blush, you sway, you flutter, and you bloom.
He, the king, majestic in burnished gold and red,
merely acknowledges,
'Yes, I see you'

Can there ever be anything between the two of you?
Lord of the universe, he the Sun,
resplendent, powerful, and relentless.

You a mere flower,
a fleeting creature,
just one of his many admirers
An ephemeral relationship at most!

By dusk, with a swish of his purple cloak,
he's gone.
You droop and weep dewy tears,
but he's going to leave you every day

Are you not done?

The remove is too infinite
There can never be a union
Why do you crave him so?
Have you not seen
the adoring many besides you?

What can there ever be between the two of you?
A mere bloom
budding today
wilting in another
desiring the Lord of the Heavens?!

You thought...
A union of spirit?
Ha!
Just a daily flirtation!
Nothing else can there ever be
Between the two of you.

Infestations

Surreptitious Secret Service Undetected by any Surveillance.

SSSUS

You might as well say.

Sssssshhhuuu

They are everywhere. We have been majorly invaded. You thought you could pay your way out of this one. No, they're in. Very, very in.

Spying, watching, worming their way in.

Pests in the kitchen are old hat. Dark red ones, the in colour, with funky hats and dressy translucent wings, they've been around. Translucent is now the rage. Ask the fashionistas.

Goatee bearded exercisers, runners, and sprinters spied anytime as they bandicoot across your vision in the garden. And your domestic pet has spied on them too; its fluffed and ruffled tail says,

'Hey you, you there, Alien!'

But all you'll see is the vanishing tail. Boy, they're fast.

Only cuter now, as stubbles and the morning-after look have caught on.

Girls like the rough chin and the hairy look, but only on their own human species.

We're exploring Mars for God's sake. The new relationships will definitely be interspecies. Think bandicoot and cat, Martian and earth girl. Let your imagination spiral out of control, earthling!

My housecat General Boosh lords over a small army!

Flying Tick Brigade, Armpit Flea Platoon, and SS Deep Fur Tick Corps, embedded in her fur, are all at her command and deployable immediately. She's made friends with her invaders much like the British colonizers with the local populace, suffering them. They came with the newly conquered territory.

An uneasy relationship, but strong.

What is an infestation? It's just an unwelcome occupier and colonizer of your space.

But the question of space starts in prehistoric times. The chicken and egg situation.

Who came here first?

The earthworms in my garden claim ancient rights, and I've been trying to evict them for years. Unsuccessfully!

They inhabit the ground just below, coming up for a breather now and then, especially on wet, muggy, rainy days. Top hatted, a little globule of squiggly earth crowning them, they wriggle up to salute me mockingly. My eyesight, not being what it used to be, but I still know they bear a mocking grin because they've been outwitting me for years. A full-bodied squirm, like a royal hand waved to the waiting plebeians, and they're back in, into my green and now pitted grass.

Now that I think of it, it might even be mooning, a wiggle of their naked arses.

I may fume, but they claim prior rights that any Court of All Creatures will uphold.

Their ground before it became mine.

I'm the infestation. The infester.

And I thought I was the lord and master of this earth.

I'm just the last of the creatures created. In line for extinction, as other arrogant infesters before me.

The big dinosaurs came and went, thundered, shook the earth, and yet, went. And so did many others after them. Came and left.

We are all occupants of this earth at one time or the other, claiming rights, denying those before us, and succumbing to the ones who are to follow. Each colonizer is an unwelcome visitor.

Our planet, our home, seems to be reeling under the effects of us colonizing multitudes that begin to think this is our home, and that we can use the earth at will, however we like. Fooled us.

Mama Earth will have the last laugh. Vermin may come, vermin will go, but no permanent pests will be tolerated.

Dinosaurs, Goatee bearded bandicoots, or humans are all here for a while, guests in what they term their home and habitat. We too.

Just Infestations.

Ek Kasak

Random thoughts while sitting in the garden. Trees and sun overhead, the Mali my gardener at work, termites in the garden to be exterminated, and a wandering mind, mine, connecting all.

Mein chai pe rahee thi
Ghar ki seeree par baith
Samnne Mali kharaa, kaam rok
Apni chai pe rahaa thaa

Chai ekathhi banee thi
Hazram ke haath ke
Meethi zordaar
Phir ......

Kuch vakt kharaa sa ho gayaa

Hawa bhi chall rahi thi
Dhoop chaon bhi bikhray thae
Baag ke aam jhool rahe thae
Phool bhi mehek, titlian urr urr

Par vakt kharaa sa ho gayyaa

Ek pal mein mainay
ehsaas kiyaa
Uunch, neech
Maali, saab
Vaytan, pagaar
Aur phir
Meraa,
teraa

Kuch vakt kharaa saa ho gayaa

Kaisay hamnay alag kar diyaa hai.
Ek doosray ko,
ek doosray se
Insaan ko, insaan se

Maalik ye kaisay karm hai?
Kiskay karm
Meray
Ke uskay?

Tunay bhi to hamay
Apne se alag kar diya hai.
Vo kiskay karm thae?
Kiske karm?
Meray,
Ya teray?

Kaun bataayaygaa?
Itni dooree kaisay
Itni unch neech?
Tu to goongaa hai
Chuppi ke kasam khaae hai.
Main bolun?
Ye baag he maalik hai
Hum sabb eskay naukar.

Ye hawa ye dhoop
Paaband nahi kiske
Hum insaan hi
aazad nahi.

Insaaniyat ko paa bhi jaayain
to, jaanvarone
Pe haave

Ab mujhay he dekh lo
Kal raat
Char motay chuhae aayay thae
Balcony mein jhagar rahey thae
Kuch khana kam paraa hogaa

Aaj ka plan hai
Unko jaan se marney ka
Zeher khilaanay ka
Baagh to unkaa bhi hai.
Insaaniyat kahan gayee?

क्यों तुम
क्यों समझाओ
मिला तुम
बालक मैं
मैं अलग क्यों
समझाओ
ममता को तरसूँ
नैयन मिलाऊँ
रूठ क्यों तुम
समझाओ
समुन्दर तुम
भटकती लहर मैं
जाती जाती
किनारा नहीं
कब तक?
बतलाओ
प्रभु तुम, नादान मैं
ऊँच नीच का रिश्ता क्यो
समझाओ
प्रश्न पर प्रश्न
उलझन बेशुमार
बेखबर कब तक रहोगे
नज़र मिलाओ, बतलाओ
जवाब नहीं
फिर भी मालिक मानूँ
क्यों
बतलाओ

Meri zammen
Teri seema
Meraa ghar
Meri sarhad
Tu panch gaz aur peechay hojaa.

Aur
Aaj ke din
Isi baag mein
hum aaj abhi chotay.
Massoom keron ko
Neem ke pani se barsaa rahe hai.
Tarpaa rahe hain

Disinfestation kaho
ya zulum
Hatya??
Kiski aankon se deko gay
Meraa meraa Meraa
Meraa teraaa....

The Grand Canyon

The Grand Canyon.

My travels

Yesterday, the 21st of May, was a most memorable day for me, a day like any other, but very special in a way. I saw the Grand Canyon in Nevada, and was completely humbled by this raw, jagged wonder of nature, one of mother Nature's greatest creations.

Early at 3.25 am, the alarm trilled, and Naresh and I got up grumpily.

We had to, because the Papillon Canyon Tours pick-up was going to come for us at an unearthly 4.25 a.m.

That was the only tour available for what we wanted to see. Ambitiously, or rather like armchair adventurists, given our advancing years and equally advancing laziness, we opted to see the canyon by airplane, helicopter, and boat.

In my younger days, I might have included whitewater rafting in the rapids of the Colorado River, some of which are rated 10 on a scale of 1–10.

The bus pick-up sped us away to Boulder City airport, a good hour away, with us and another fifteen tourists of different ages and ethnicities.

The airport was asleep; it's coffee and gift shop visible through the shutters, being readied to serve us. We presented ourselves, got our boarding passes, and had two silver stickers, pinned American-style, on our fronts saying, 'Grand Voyager 'and 'Skywalk'.

In the meantime, I noticed two sides to this tiny airport, a tarmac where small ancient airplanes were parked, and the other with shiny red helicopters.

In an hour, or more, the airport filled up with about 70–80 people. All booked on slightly different tours around the main attraction, the Grand Canyon.

Time for departure. Our silver stickers, 'Grand Voyager and Skywalk', got called out by a handsome first officer. We found fellow mates and followed the first officer to our aircraft. The Grand Canyon Airlines aircraft was of 1969 vintage.

The canyon was a million years old and still being made by Mother Nature. By comparison, a very young captain whom we now met, at least 70 years old, was going to fly us into the valley.

In his able hands, ensconced in the sturdy craft, we flew away. I could see the controls, old-fashioned dials, and joysticks in the cockpit through the open door.

My headphones on, I heard what we were seeing below through a commentary.

In the early morning light, it was 7.30 am, a bit cloudy, over the Sierra Nevada mountains and desert, our eyes were glued to the large picture windows. Cameras, cell phones, and iPads were all clicking away at the vistas, even before the eyes made contact with the wonders of nature. After the picture taking, then to see, actually see, second hand, belatedly.

We passed over the great Hoover Dam, built in 1939. The heaviest man-made cement structure in the world. Colorado's waters are harnessed and stored in Lake Mead for users as far as California. The blue waters of the river enter the lake in jagged channels, set amid the barren and brown land of the Sierra Nevada mountains.

And us, in the whirring, deafening propeller plane, the propeller in my line of vision, high above the brown and blue serenity below, not a tree or green bush in sight.

Along with a smiling Australian couple in the late eighties. Who with lined faces looked at each other with endearing love, which needed no conversation, just togetherness.

Along with an Indian family of four from south India, chattering away in Tamil, the father with a large zoom camera around his neck and a huge tablet phone.

A spritely daughter with a headband festooned with two bobbing paper roses, like a special antenna the young have on, had her own camera; another, a sleepy younger child who occupied a window seat and wasted it away on childlike slumber, and a wife who did nothing but herd the brood.

Another family from a neighbouring state, sitting far away and not within my radar of notice.

Then a young Gujrati couple from Mumbai, bouncing around gaily, the pink wife with blue shades happily posing all the time, to be photographed by her equally pink and plump husband.

So many Indians, all wanderlust driven.

Our flight landed at the helicopter base on the rim of the canyon. We transferred to one along with the young couple, now our newly made friends from Mumbai, and took off.

The Grand Canyon valley, all too familiar seen in pictures and posters, looked less spectacular, brown and grey in the dull early morning light, with its characteristic stratified layers and flat peakless rims, appearing in every direction as we flew.

The short helicopter flight landed us at the canyon bottom.

We looked up all around at the wonder, the wonder that had yet to awe us with its awesomeness.

Many young guides aided us from helicopter to boat, all young Native Americans, descendants of the first occupants of this ancient land.

Looking so serious in their uniforms, probably weighed down by their ancient past and histories. Down a short, steep slope into a motorized boat. We, in our red life jackets, now continued our exploration of the majestic canyon on the Colorado River.

Heedless of our personal opinions, the canyon unfolded itself, bend after bend of the river. Eyes rose up to see steep sides, coming down to the now muddy waters.

Only fish, no crocodiles or snakes, were the inhabitants of its waters, explained our boat guide, the lad from the Hualipai Native Indian tribe. The land on the left belonged to the tribe, and the land on the right to the American nation, he added. Ironic, that it was conceded to the ancient tribals by the new, invading usurpers

The land of the canyon was old and had seen the torture of many geological forces, of a young, reckless river carving its valley, of erosion and weathering by fierce winds and hot desert heat. And of slow, rigorous mountain building, another kind of tyranny of the mighty upon the old earth.

Divisions, strife and cruelty everywhere, in nature as among people.

PLANE FLYING OVER THE GRAND CANYON

Grand Voyage over, now the last part of the journey awaited us: the Skywalk, certainly an engineering feat!

The Skywalk projected out of the rim of the canyon, a horseshoe-shaped glass platform, created for voyeurs to be transported to adrenalin highs.

Feet encased in protective fabric caps covering the shoes, so as not to scratch the glass surface, we came upon the Skywalk. To find we were walking right into space with the deep, sheer drop of the canyon below, hundreds of feet down, like nothing to stop us from falling through except a few sheets of glass, propped on metal scaffolding.

Now my heart in my mouth, I retracted my earlier words. I absolutely did not want the curse of the proud canyon upon me. The Grand Canyon enfolded itself, awesome from every angle. It spread itself out in all its magnificent formations, just indescribable. The Sun out by this time, the hues of sunlight now warmer, the Grand Canyon began turning a richer gold and red, speaking to us from its every majestic rock. Its beauty held us spellbound; I did not want to leave.

Driven back by bus to the airport, we thanked the captain, who makes ten flights daily. I saw, at the end of our flight to Boulder City, how he meticulously entered the log, peering closely at his columns of figures. We thanked the first officer, who brought the ladder for us to descend, watching how he encased the propeller blade with a leather sheath and anchored it to the body of the plane, so that it would not rotate with the idle wind.

The motley crowd of tourists that we were, having paid homage to nature's great wonder, humbled, and now tired by the days ferrying around, devoid of chatter, quietly boarded the bus, slumbered, and finally trundled back to our hotels.

The Mighty Canyon darkened itself for the night, to await, suffer, or delight another load of gawping humans for the next day.

The Art Corridor

An Oorja art show curated by MG Doddamani

During the Oorja Feb 24, 2020 exhibition in the Taj Westend Art Corridor, a group of senior artists, along with the upcoming Oorja art group, exhibited their works.

Late evenings before closing became very quiet.

We all took turns to be there, to receive visitors who flocked for this successful ten day long show, kept company by the pigeons from the lush Westend Hotel forest.

In the Art Corridor
No one is here but me
And...
Two pregnant pigeons
Guarding their little ones
overhead, on the beam with light
Cooing with delight
You see, they've nested there
Do you think the hotel staff care?

The Art Corridor In Western Hotel Oorja 2020

They do, yes they do
Won't destroy their nests
After all, they're hotel guests
Pigeons keep dropping their poo
Little plops of brown goo
Staff keep it clean
Wipe the floor
Then preen
It's gone, Ma'am
Now, from the chandelier swinging
Cheep, cheep, coo, coo, singing
But
Where are all the art lovers?
They need to see these pics
Before they go back
In their plastic covers

They'll look swell on someone's wall
So, guys, give your friends a call
Remind them to come
One and all.

Printed Black

Another interesting art class, learning to print our artwork, course work for our Bachelor's degree in fine art.

Linocut day found Vanaja, Kanti, Jyoti and me slicing away with our sharp blades, our chosen beasts or birds, on Lino sheets in the studio. Vanaja scratched away a grizzly bear, Kanti, a pair of hens, and Jyoti, a bird.

Next day, the work was printed. I forgot to take my linocut Zebra home after printing.

In fact, I never found him again. But the Zebra had his own thoughts about this class.

Plucked me out of my jungle
Photographed away
Put me on paper
Copied today.

Then transferred me to Lino
And scratched my bum away
Blackened and printed
The very next day.

A guy has some shame
But these artists
Have none
Fiddling fadling with my bum
just for their kind of weird fun.

In my forest, I knew Simba, Bambi, and Ka,
Here none
That fat hag
Could have taken me
In her bag.

But she lost me here
In another kind of forest
A studio,
they call it.

So bare
No friends, no trees, no water, or grass
Just paper, paint, pictures,
and a vase.

I'm bereft without friends
So sad
They're all I had
Someone, please find me
and send me home.

LINOCUT ZEBRA

I'm a stripey kind of guy
with four legs, I don't fly,
kinda shy
But I'm lost under all
this artist's stuff.

In Africa, my home, I could run
But printed on paper
Has taken out the fun
Stiff, plastered with black paint
Gosh, my old lady would faint.

My striped hide
All messy and sticky
My tail
No more, flicky
A shame!

But what's my name?
A Zebra, Equus Quagga
The scientists say
Like a donkey? A horse?
Telling these nincompoops
In the studio today.

You like your jungle
I mine
Each to his own

In My Jungle, Hey, Look At My Socks!

Send me home
I'm so alone.

The painted mare
With long, silky hair
Her bum sliced away
She's too snooty.

Besides,
she's high up on the wall
I'm on the floor
In newspapers, astray.

The hen from the farm
Lent for the day
Though the farmer meant no harm
Wings plastered
She's drying on the line today.

The grizzly
No pot of honey to steal
No flies to swat from that meal
Not a tree to scratch
Himself, frozen away.

The bird on the stump
Though her wings aren't clipped
Won't take off today

In black and white
You have us in print
You won't capture us
in line or spirit.

Our fur won't fluff
Our tails won't swish
Our eyes will be dull
Our bodies won't throb.

You won't fall in love
With the guy from the forest
He ain't there
In the studio bare.

Pearls

For Neetu, when she sent the extraordinary picture of raindrops on the plant.

It rained all night
See,
I made a string of pearls
On the green vine
Claimed the Rain
Interjected the Vine
The creation is mine
I held the delicate droplets
Around my neck

He laughed.

And told Rain and Vine
I made you both
Made the red sunset
The perfect wave

Neetu, then,
He looked at you

Pearl Drops

Picture Of The Previous Night's Rain As Taken By Nitu

I made
The air you breathe
Your little baby's hand
Your mother's face
I made the man who was Buddha

Let me take you
On a journey divine
Hold my hand
And you can paint my wonders
And etch them in time

I'll merge into your canvas
I'll steal into your paint
I'll be there in spirit
And line

Time after time
I'll come and go
Hold my hand
And you'll always be fine

Not a word was spoken
Uttered or said
Just a sense in your heart
That was all that was said

Aagay Jaakay ....

Guru ka Dera

The Art Studio, Our Haven

Aagay jaakay
Kuch sunaayee degaa
kuch dekhaai dega
Kuch samajh rahaygee
kuch saans bechae hongay

Nahi to kaisay mein
haatho ko rangon se rangoongee?
Tasveero mein
rang kaisay bharungee?

Meray suryasth kaisay
kabhi asth na hongay?
Meray uunth kaisay
raygisthan mein mast rahengay?

Mein kaisay vehh
uunchee seeri charrhungee
Jahaan meray guru ka dera hai?
Us rangeen duniya mein
meray doston ka baseraa hai

Dost

Neetu, Neelam, Dr Venkatraman, M. G. Doddamani, Ritu, Vanaja, Jyoti, Kanti

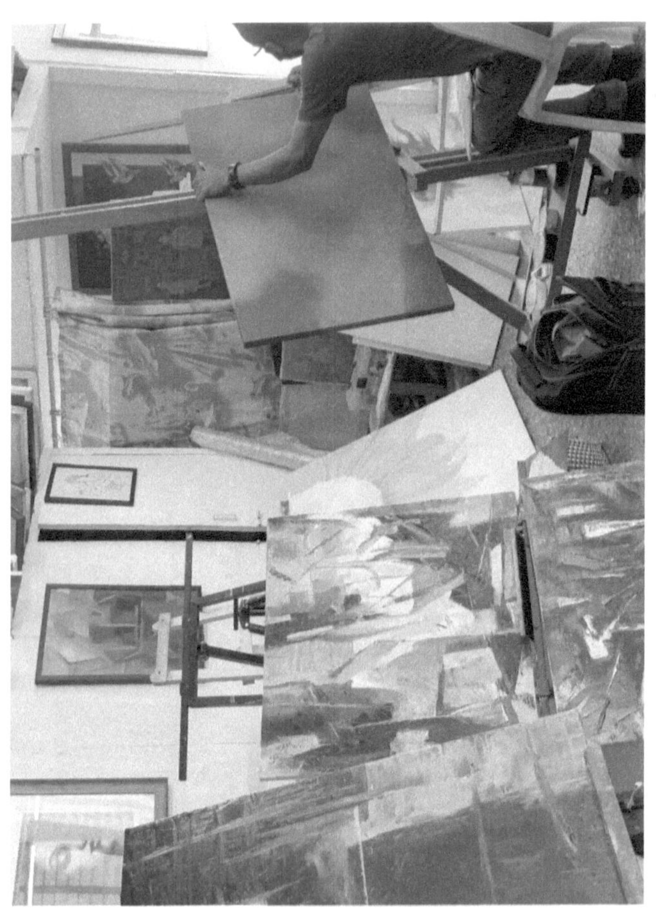

STUDIO

Aatay jaatay
Aatay jaatay hain
Kabhi Rosh, kabhi Ritu
Kabhi Vanaja, kabhi Nitu
Door se Jyoti
Paas se Kanti

Azeez bahut hai sab
Dost hain meray
Sab ki apni apni duniya hai
Chorr ke aatay hain
Kaagaz pe holi khelnay
Bahut azeez hai mujhko.

Sunnanaa, dehknaa, samajhna
mahsoos karna
Haathon paaon ka chalna
Hota rahe
Hum seeri charrtay rahain.
Bas aatay jaatay rahein.

Unche unche manzilon tak
Meray doston ka pahunchna hota rahey
Bahut karr liyay
dhakkaaa mukki, maraa maree
Ab to lutf ka vakt hai

Chund kuch samay bacha hai
Aadhay kaan, ek aankh
Langri taang, uljhi saans,
Inse hi kaam chalaa lengay

Uncee seeri charr lengay
Guru ka dera na chodaygay
Aatay jaatay....Aagay jaatay
Rahen gay.

My Secret Garden

Sitting alone
With the world inside my heart
Just the whirring fan
For conversation
The Booch downstairs
Not lending her presence
Sleepy albeit
But a warm, throbbing being
And mine by force

I'm often sitting alone
At airports
Before the canvas
The newspaper
My busy loved ones
one by one, flooding my heart
I love them
Live them
The swell and the wane
in the ocean of my heart
Whole stories and conversations
With nothing said
All in a world of my own

What I cannot say
Not allowed nor welcome
It peeps out hesitantly
Now it's there, and now it's gone
Plays hide and seek
In the memory of
My Secret Garden
I live, Papa does, Nishu, Nazu
Gau and Jo, Miru
Now Tooti Frooti ooooooo
Oh, this secret garden
Is my delightful world.
I play like a child
In the boundless sunshine
And colours galore
It's picnic bed covers and cushions
And little ones tumbling all over
Is where I live
Hugs and kisses
Magical love, sweetness, and more...
My Secret Garden...

Tooti Frooti is Jona. Booch is our beloved cat. This was penned before the advent of Zar, Tara and Anika.

Prince and Princess

When Jo and Gau came for Tanaaz's wedding in 2019. This poem is for the two doctors, my children.

Sheets yanked off
Pillows plumped
Towels in the wash
Blankets in the Sun.

The children have left
The nest is empty
Boochie is lonely
Sulking under the table.

Two days
The house had chatter
Noise and fun
There was laughter.

Laptops winking
Fingers typing
so much homework
Doctors mugging

They've gone
As they always do
Back to their lives
Far, far away

The old father, silent
Went to work
The old mother stored
The memories away

They'll come again
That's how we live
With hope in our hearts
The phone close by

Our kitchen will cook off
Dishes galore
The table will invite
With fruit and more

Our servants will run
To do their bidding
The prince is home
With Princess in tow

For now, he's gone
Princess by his side
Taken the sunshine
Stars and all

They'll come again
Prince and Princess
He'll bring the sunshine
She'll carry the stars

Mother's heart will burst
With joy and pride
To see such two
Blessed and fine

Keep It Safe

FOR TONI AND KAVITA

The little haven
of peace and love
that you have created
and call your home
is a blessed place
Keep it safe.

The generous table
Of strawberries and figs
Of almonds and grapes
Delicious foods
Prepared by yourself
You share with all
Keep it safe.

Your strong belief
Humble faith
In God alone and His will
Of sharing and caring
Compassion for all
Keep it safe.

Be blessed.
with His Bounty
May it more than rain
Be a deluge instead
Of His Gifts Galore
Health, laughter, and love
Keep it safe.

I pray.
He may hear me
And concede
The same
Keep you as his children
Indulged Spoilt Innocent
and safe.

Words to Jo

WHEN CARRYING
TIMTUM, MY GRANDDAUGHTER

You are far and yet
Close to my heart
You don't say
Yet I know you feel a lot.
You want to be with
Your home and child
Yet I know
Your work calls you.

Because you are so sincere
And caring
You neglect yourself
But not those you heal.

I know, I know
Maybe I know
Some of it's wrong
But I can sense
Some and more

I wish and wish for you
That you may have
Time with your handsome son
And the other who dotes on you
My handsome son

May you see Jona
In mischief and in learning
In growing
In blossoming

Your mother's heart
rejoice
Be filled with joy to
The brim

For we have Miss Cupcakes coming
For her Mommy's care
She will look at you
You'll melt, I know

You must be dreaming
Of bows and ribbons
Pinks and florals
Baby dresses

May you have all the gifts
Of life
May you see your family
Be before your eyes

I wish you health
Happiness and more...
Your heart's desires
And your dreams coming true.

Hugs
Love
And blessings
From a mother

Ma

Gone My Love

For my Father Kanwarbhan Bhatia

1921 – 2012

That one, the day, that was,
of goodbyes
is now no more.
Just melted, like it was never there.
Like ice cream, licked clean
Off the cone
And then the cone itself,
Never there.
Memories fade if you don't nurture them
People are just gone,
gone even if you hold them tight.

The tighter you grip,
The looser it gets
They're gone
Before your very eyes
The names, endearments, and titbits remain
The loved one just wafts away with the breeze.
He's gone to a new land

It pains not there
Our cruelty unknown.
Love of my life, you were right
To run away
It pains, you're not here
It would pain more, if you were
To see you hurt,

Rather, I hurt
Than you
So, fly away, my love
You did right
So happy, it hurts you no more.

That day, you went
Etched deep and bright
I saw you in that morning light
On ice, that ice was you
Frozen, handsome slumbering

No goodbyes,
That's good.
No closure for me,
I'll treasure you forever more.

(Dad was on a block of ice outside the morgue of
Gangaram Hospital when I saw him upon reaching
Delhi.)

Beloved of Krishna

Monday mornings were always reserved for Gita class in Pinky Baljee's house with Swami Haridasji. We heard him recite for 25 years and studied several Vedic texts, besides the Gita with him.

It was a class like no other, one which we did not like to miss, with a teacher so gentle and yet profound that we never felt we were being taught. In retrospect it was reverential to be with him.

Written when Swami Haridasji became very ill after a fall.

The man who was
My Guru
You were that
And now you are
Him who is close
So close
Just a breath away
From his own
Very own Krishna

The loss is mine
for I thought
You were forever
Ours
But
You were in waiting
Waiting
For the call
Ready
To surrender into His arms
And he too...
Krishna,
waiting,
For his beloved son
You.

The call is yet to come
And you are saying your goodbyes

Books to your erudite pupil,
And gifts
from your Father to yourself,
bequeathed already
To an undeserving another
Thanking all
Leaving none
even for the love
Showered on you.

What can we give you?
We, the beggars
Came to you
Mindless
You taught us to be mindful.
What can we offer?

You expounded
Scriptures, mantras, and mahavakayas
Divinity, pure love
The essence
Oneness.........
You expounded
Your words dripped, honey
We hung on, in love, enslaved.

You are beloved of Him
Krishna
What can we give, but
Send you with
Raised hands
In prayer
May you be received
As you have always hoped
Like a son, come home
Home
To his father's home

Away, this fumbling,
this hesitant gait,
you are absorbed in Him,
impatient to be merged,
and barely spare us
a phrase or two.
But when you do,
It is a pearl majestic
As only my own teacher's be

I grudge you not,
I will miss you.
Forever and ever
No one I have ever known
Like you.

You are alone
By yourself
On a pedestal
I bow.

But I love you
Like a child
For you were always
Him
Krishna
Love itself,

Swami Haridas Ji

Never above
Or far removed from our
Ordinariness.

Held our hand
Shaped our minds
Thought our thoughts
Murmured
'Love the Lord,
Krishna '.

Whence would I have heard
What you expounded
Miserable creatures us
But for your love
Would have remained thus.
Miserable.

I wish you well
In His arms, may you be received
Godspeed
Gently, like a fresh flower
Arrive at his doorstep.
Godspeed
Like a fresh flower.

No more words
Just breath.

Krishna
Krishnaa
Krishnaaa.

Swami became one with his very own Krishna on July
30th, 2024.
Swami Haridasji: October 2nd, 1939 - July 30th, 2024.

Abbu

In our family you never asked about Abbu, her father. It was taboo to speak of him for the pain was still palpable, his mother's, his wife's, his sisters', his two brothers'.

The two little girls he left behind, two and three years old were unaware, oblivious of their loss.

Her father
But he left her
She knew him not
How could he?
How could he?

She was too small
He knew
She didn't
She hadn't said hello
He finished goodbyes.

Deep in her mother's bosom
The suckling infant
Had found him not
Knew him not
Not yet.

Just learnt to hold her mother's thumb
Trust her smells and her flesh
Her father
She knew him not
Too soon, he flew away.

In his pain, he knew not
The pain of the other
He caused.

Her mother's
Her's
And her sister's
Small

He left them
For the promise false.
Of a land
Sorrowless
Painless

There is no such land
Whence we would go
There is no such land
Strifeless or utopian.

We are born to hurt
We live, we hurt
We die, we hurt.

Like fools, we laugh
With gay abandon
We forget or try
Yet we hurt.

Are we fools or unwise?
The brightest of God's creation
When will we know?

Hurt not,
sorrow not,
weep not.
It's just His play
Of toys, big and small.

But I can't forget
He left her
Fatherless
She was so small.

Yet to ask
Abbu?

For what?

For whom?

Was it better there?

Abbu?

Abbu took his own life. In the dead of night, Grandmother heard a pistol shot in her room. She rushed to find her son, the eldest, in a pool of blood, dead. And as children we were never told why.

Raj

MY DIDI
More beautiful today than ever before!

The depth of a wonderful life well lived gives you radiance, enduring confidence, and strength.

Your calm gaze (never mind the one unseeing eye) and your happy smile (red lipstick zindabad, how many sticks have you gone through?), ever a welcome for all.

Didi, you haven't changed at all.

The brightest star among the ever-vocal, ever-opinionated Bhatia girls, you stand tall. I think it would be appropriate to say tall and statuesque.

It's understandable, Padma can't stand tall. She may be sexy and cute, but all of four feet nothing cannot stand tall! Impossible!! Rock and roll perhaps.

Some of us are rather on the wide side, like me, and Radhe, so we can't stand tall; some of us have rickety knees, or did till recently, like Babe, so can barely stand. Some are always bouncing around, from Goa to Rishikesh, like Gulla; they can't stand in one place, leave alone stand tall.

RAJ

Some aren't even all themselves; what about transplanted body parts from husbands?!

Didi, you were always ahead, always an achiever, and easily a leader, but the most unassuming and humblest among us all.

While writing this, my mind played games

What if you were the eldest son of the family? What if you had studied abroad (which you weren't allowed) and come back even more educated? What if you had joined the diplomatic services and had a position in public?

I think you would have carved out a successful path anywhere.

I can picture you in each and all of these roles.

You know why?

You give your best, you work the hardest, and you don't get bogged down with ego and attitude. You never stop learning.

Didi, you're an example, if only we could follow.

But far from being perfect, perfect people can be distant and cold. You are adorable. We each love you; we fight over you, and we are jealous of your affections. Radha squabbles with Sharan and Neelam with Baby because we love you and want you to love us most of all.

Nose Chomper

One morning in March 2020, at eight months old, Jona got his first two teeth.

When Gautam went to pick him up, he bit his nose.

Littlu Bittlu, you bit my son
You son of a gun
You bit my son
On his nose
You bit my son.

You better learn to run
Coz I'm going to catch you
And when I do
I'm going to bite your bum.

Littlu Bittlu
It's going to be fun
Running after you
And chomping at your bum.

JONA THE NOSE CHOMPER

I can't get over it
You bit your dad
Who does that?
Naughty boy
Bad, bad, bad.

Kya Dhoondtaa Hai Bawra

Kya Dhoondtaa Hai Bawra?
Aaj ki shaam bhi
Tamaam hui
Yeh roz ki kahani hai
Jaisa ek shahir ne kaha hai

Subah hoti hai, shaam hoti hai
Jindagi yoon he tamaam hoti hai

Rozgaari ki
Talaash mein insaan
Waqt ko keemti samajh
Rehta hai din raat pareshaan

Mainay kya hain meri zindagi ke
Kyon paidaa hua,
Kyon zinda hoon,
Dhundtaa hai wajay, subah shaam.

Koi sandhya ki neelee siyahi mein
Guru ke charno mein mathaa rakh
Aur
Koi parvardigaar to yaad kar
Dhun mein rehtaa hai mast

Sab musafir
Waqt kaat rahe hain
Samay bitaa rahe hain

Kab kisnay kuch vasool kiyaa?
Kya mila?
Koi vajai?
Kab kisnay kabool kiyaa?

Koi ketaabon mein dhoondtaa hai maksad
Fakir insaano mein bantaa hai farishtaa
Rozgaari se nahi fursat garib ko
Aur manmaani main mast, amir

Waqt guzaartain hai sab mehmaan
Chund din ke liya aayay
Naasamajh, bhool jata hai
Aaj aayay,
aur kal
Jaana bhi hai

Ye waqt
Kambakht waqt,
kat taa he nahi
Shaam guzarti he nahi

Bhool bhuliyaa mein uljhaa
Zindagi ke rangon mein rangaa
Ek din thak jayaygaa
Reh jaayagaa hairaan

Nahi milay gaa maksad
Har mor par, ek aur mor
Titliyon ko pakartaa rahegaa
Urr, urr, jaayain gee
Haath na aayain gee

Yon ka tyon rah jaayaygaa
Pareshaan hairaan

Miti ka madho
Jaisa beh rahaa hai daryaa
Beh jaayaygaa
Yeh insaan

Phir Bawra
kyaa Aur kyun
dhundtaa hai?

Waiting for You

Krishna
Are you waiting for me
'Coz
I'm certainly waiting for you
Got nowhere to go
Only have your address
Vague
Unnumbered
How will I find you?
Well, then
You find me
I'm dregs?
But yours
Be waiting
Got nowhere else to go
Krishna
Come
Take me
I'm waiting
Don't show it
Or know it
But I'm homeless
Got no one here

KRISHNA BY MY WINDOW

Be always
Waiting for you
Lord
Resting in you
Waiting
It's fine
I'll be waiting
I know
You'll come